HARAMACY

ZAHED SULTAN
PRESENTS

HARAMACY

EDITED BY
DHRUVA BALRAM • TARA JOSHI

unbound

First published in 2022

Unbound
Level 1, Devonshire House, One Mayfair Place,
London W1J 8AJ
www.unbound.com

© COMMUN, 2022

Text design by Ellipsis, Glasgow

A CIP record for this book is available from the British
Library

ISBN 978-1-80018-132-8 (paperback)
ISBN 978-1-80018-133-5 (ebook)

Printed and bound in Great Britain by
Clays Ltd, Elcograf S.p.A

1 3 5 7 9 8 6 4 2

Najat Sultan   Fawzia Sultan

A special thank you to F.M.S. who generously supported our first collection of stories and dedicates their contribution to Najat Hamad Sultan Bin Isa and Fawzia Hamad Sultan Bin Isa.

Both women died at a young age, however they left a footprint that surpassed their lifetime in the articles of Kuwait's History.

Najat was driven to empower women to have a voice, tirelessly advocating for their rights and pushing through barriers to achieve equal opportunity. Najat contributed to the Arts by championing Sadu House, a not-for-profit initiative that nurtured traditional weaving techniques by Bedouin women and working alongside her brother Ghazi at the Sultan Gallery to showcase emerging artists from the region

Fawzia, on the other hand, focused on improving the education landscape in Kuwait and established a not-for-profit, bilingual institute in 1977, Al Bayan School. Committed to early childhood development, Fawzia instilled ideals of critical thinking and breaking the status quo to realise one's true potential and play a role in bettering society.

Najat and Fawzia didn't succeed without numerous failures and life experiences, teaching us valuable lessons in how to shape one's identity and place value in contributing to your community.

HARAMACY

НАНАМАСУ

CONTENTS

Foreword Zahed Sultan   ix

1 A ROADMAP TO SURVIVING
   EMOTIONAL AND PROFESSIONAL
   HEARTBREAK
   Aina J. Khan   1

2 THE BALLAD OF THE KANGAROO
   BANDIT
   Joe Zadeh   15

3 SHELTER IN PLACE
   Sanjana Varghese   29

4 THE SHALLOWS
   Nasri Atallah   43

5 THE ILLEGITIMATE INDIAN
   Cyrine Sinti   63

6 ON BEING LOUD
   Ammar Kalia   79

7   WHO OWNS A STORY?
    Saleem Haddad   95

8   MY LOVE IS VAST, BUT SO IS MY
    DIFFERENCE
    Nouf Alhimiary   119

9   ON SAYING GOODBYE
    Tara Joshi   129

10 GARY IS NOT MY NAME
    Dhruva Balram   145

11 REST
    Kieran Yates   161

Epilogue Zahed Sultan   183
Editors' note   189
Contributors' biographies   193
Notes   197
Supporters   203

FOREWORD
ZAHED SULTAN

It's Thursday, 2 August 1990. I wake up early in
the morning to the sound of water gushing from
metal taps. Both the bathtub and the sink are
being filled to the brim in the bathroom of the
room I share with my younger brother. Confused,
I drag myself downstairs with my brother to look
for my father. I look outside, and in the court-
yard, I see my mother's oversized ornamental pots
being topped up, with rice? Adding to my confusion, other essentials are being stockpiled in pecu-
liar places. My father sees us, holds our hands
and takes us outside the front door to our house.
In the distance we see military tanks in formation
on the roundabout nearby. The cars usually
circling it and diverting onto busy streets are at a
standstill. This once agitated early-morning com-
mute is now a serene, octopus-like parking lot
with tentacles of cars extending as far as the eye
can see.

This is my earliest memory of the Iraqi invasion of Kuwait.

As confused as my brother and I were at the time, there was a silver lining. The night before, my father had taken us out to buy our first Nintendo gaming console (*Mario Kart* included). What's more, he had also retrieved two of his prized watches from the shop where they'd been repaired.

I experienced about thirty days of the nine-month Iraqi occupation of Kuwait. Fragments from this time are still etched into my memory. My brother and I escaped the country one sandy afternoon through an unmarked desert route in a convoy of SUVs and family vans packed with distant relatives and elderly strangers. It took us four attempts on four separate occasions to flee Kuwait and cross the desert into Saudi Arabia. Each attempt had its complications, one of which involved being shot at by Iraqi soldiers.

We had lunch on newspapers with the Saudi border guards the day we escaped and at night slept in an empty house on mattresses on the floor. The next morning, we continued our drive to Bahrain. Eventually my brother and I flew to

London to be reunited with my mother and elder brother, both of whom had been on vacation in Thailand and found themselves stranded when Kuwait was invaded. Soon after, we travelled together to Delhi while my father remained in Kuwait to protect our home.

I never wanted to leave Kuwait, I wanted to stay with my father. But he insisted. Six months later, he too fled the country with my grandmother on a beat-up bus through Baghdad. They used false identities, pretending to be expat Indians, as they were free to return home during the occupation. He soon joined us in Delhi, where my parents had bought a flat in a new building, which was almost ready to move into. We were reunited with my father thanks to insulin, or a lack of it (he was a diabetic and ran out of his meds, urging him to escape). Although the Iraqi occupation lasted only nine months, we lived in Delhi for two years. My mother insisted we did because of the black smog that encapsulated Kuwait's skies from the raging oil wells set ablaze by Saddam Hussein.

Most of my childhood memories from before the occupation are happy ones. I had nurtured a close group of friends from kindergarten, did exceptionally well in school, and was enamoured for the first time, at a distance, by a new girl who had joined our sixth-grade class.

However, my memories are also riddled with irregularities. I remember one instance, on parent-teacher day, where classmates nudged me to join them in laughing at a lady wearing an intricately laced *sari* with a pronounced *bindi* on her forehead. I chose to stay quiet. Or another instance, during an after-school sports match, when a classmate pointed to a peculiar-looking man with big, curly hair and a thick beard sitting cross-legged on the tiered benches of the gym wearing a *dishdasha* (the national dress). I pretended I couldn't see.

This lady and this man were my parents. I was born to an Indian mother and a Kuwaiti father. They were introduced to each other through mutual friends in Bombay (Mumbai). My late father's fluency in speaking Hindi surpassed his ability to speak Arabic, mostly because the formative years of his upbringing were spent in India with his brothers and sisters. At the time, this was normal. It was even celebrated to have close ties with the Indian subcontinent among merchant families through trade and commerce. But somehow, post-oil, Kuwait's relationship with India changed; they brought labourers to the country in droves from India and marginalised them by limiting their rights and offering them substandard wages to do the menial work Kuwait's new elite thought beneath them.

Still, despite the pronounced divisions, I was able to navigate my dual upbringing with relative confidence.

Before the age of ten, I used to practise reading the Quran. So much so, I won a gold medal in a government-led Quran-reading competition for my skills in *tilawa* (recitation). I remember coming home that day from school to be greeted by a big banner of 'Congratulations!' with balloons hovering mid-air. Loud applause and cheers of joy emanated from my parents and a new bicycle awaited me as a reward for my achievement. News of my win spread quickly through family circles (which are fairly large). I was praised as 'the gifted one' and showered with blessings of grace in Arabic: *mashallah!* (god willing). Thereafter, during family gatherings and hospital visits to see elders, I was instructed to recite a *soura* (verse) from the Quran on demand. Folding my arms and lowering my head in submission, I did what was asked. Unbeknownst to me at the time, this is where my abilities as a performer began to take shape.

Growing up, an amalgamation of traditions and religious rituals melded together naturally at home. Sunday nights were open-house for *chaat*, bite-sized Indian street food, and Wednesdays were reserved for Peking duck, a family favourite. We sang *Om Jai Jagdish Hare* for Diwali, the Indian festival of light, and *The Twelve Days of Christmas* for seasonal yuletides under an ornately decorated family tree. Curiously, Ramadan, the fasting month for Muslims, was not observed at home. I insisted on fasting, though, waking up at the crack of dawn to eat *Suhur* before the *Fajir* prayer. To this day, more often than not, I fast during Ramadan. I can't say why exactly; maybe it's a force of habit or a deeply ingrained faith in the divine? What I can say is that murmurs of the word *haram* (forbidden) still echo in my mind from the days of religion class at school or the fear of being called *Kalb Ramadan* (the dog of Ramadan) by friends and cousins if you were caught not fasting.

Straddling two cultures comes naturally to me. I have done it my whole life, developing an elasticity to stretch and mould into complementary, at times conflicting spaces.

Exploring the idiosyncrasies of cultures while celebrating their similarities can create a interlocking space that feels like home. I have experienced first-hand how cross-cultural interactions can lead to ingenuity and acceptance. If we consider our world today, we can see that overcoming social injustice can't be achieved by dividing communities through perceived identities, but rather by coming together and untangling the hidden threads that exist between different groups.

So, we give you this book. A collection of stories prescribed by voices from the Middle East, South Asia and the diaspora, unpacking their personal experiences as they learn(ed) to assimilate into a society that they chose, were born or thrust into to make their home. Tackling issues like visibility, invisibility, love, strength, resilience, race, friendship and relationships, this book highlights the various shades that make up who we are as a community.

Can this collection of stories dismantle legacy structures? Ideologies that instigate societal divides or pedagogies that perpetuate racism? Probably not. But storytelling is a universal tool that we can use to unearth pervasive issues and encourage meaningful dialogue.

Through telling my story, and sharing a space with a community of storytellers to do the same, we can ignite an understanding for those of us who felt othered and the many of us who learn to tread the tightropes of the places and people we call home. ☽

A ROADMAP TO SURVIVING EMOTIONAL AND PROFESSIONAL HEARTBREAK
AINA J. KHAN

'Remove your top, please.'

After six months of back and forth between hospital emergency departments with chest pains, a fantastically stubborn infection, weight loss, a persistent cough, and no conclusive results, my GP finally struck gold on a routine check-up; a small lump had infiltrated its way into my breast. It was the telltale sign of nothing or something.

I was due to fly out on a month-long work trip and combined holiday the very next morning. The choice was simple: go topless in front of the robotic male doctor for a mammogram, or carry the burden of not knowing until I returned.

The sudden urge to laugh at the absurdity of the situation swept over me as I sat on the navy-blue hospital bed. My hands felt like anchors, pulling sluggishly at each end of my hijab, resting on my shoulders as if by deliberately slowing down I could avoid having to strip. The corners of my mouth drooped in passive protest, and I reluctantly undressed, raising my arms above my head. The doctor wanted to check my lymph nodes just to be safe. He squirted the cold ultrasound gel against my skin as though he were shooting a toy water-gun. Digging the device deep into my armpit, he scrutinised the black and white images on the screen behind.

'There's a slight abnormality in one of your lymph nodes,' he said. 'I'll need to take a small sample so we can test it. There's a chance I won't be able to extract enough cells. If that's the case, we'll have to schedule a biopsy when you get back.'

My thoughts wandered to the lamb's eyeball I'd dissected in school eleven years ago. Thinking of the way it had stared in unlidded terror as I prodded the corneal gel gleefully with a metal scalpel, I wondered if I had the same look of naked horror as the needle disappeared into my underarm. I screwed my eyes shut and tried to imagine the cerulean Caribbean Sea of Negril in west Jamaica that my nurse, a Jamaican woman herself, had spoken to me about earlier.

'I spent four months as a breast surgeon – 99 per cent of this stuff in under 35/40s is non-sinister,' a doctor friend had messaged me reassuringly. But ever the optimist, one thought lingered in my mind as the robot doctor rummaged the needle around grotesquely:

What if it was cancer?

I grew up in west London at the turn of the 1990s, when the term 'British Muslim' hadn't been widely adopted by the Muslim community. As a state-educated, first-generation graduate, raised by a single-parent mother who relied on state benefits and free school dinners, I was the poster-child for social mobility. But very early on, as a young, naive journalist starting out, I had subconsciously inter-nalised the Thatcherite mantra of meritocracy. If I just worked hard enough, collected more academic credentials under my belt, got more bylines, I would succeed. If it wasn't working out, there was something deficient in me.

And so, I concluded that if I completed a jour-nalism diploma alongside the part-time master's I was already halfway through (all while working a full-time job), and found I still couldn't get a permanent full-time journalism job, only then could I quit, knowing I had tried everything. It was as though qualifications and accolades could provide a lifejacket that would keep my head above the violent waters of a melanin-phobic industry keen on promoting 'diversity of ideas', when what it needed was diversity of authority, faces and lived experiences.

Constantly drifting from one freelance contract to another, through unpaid work-experience placements, internships, and well-meaning positive action schemes, completing applications for entry-level jobs four years into freelancing, I was struggling immensely to keep afloat, both financially and mentally.

By now, I felt like I should have been planting firmer roots with my journalism career, but the more I tried, the louder the crippling voice of imposter syndrome whispered in my ear. Maybe if I exploited the privilege of my fair skin, removed my hijab, anglicised my name to 'Anna' and masqueraded as a racially ambiguous woman, I could escape the limitations of 'diversity', that nine-letter word that has metamorphosed into a taxonomy of the human species for those with an ounce of melanin in their skin. And so I began doubting why I wanted to pursue journalism. In his advice to writers published in *The Writer's Chapbook: A Compendium of Fact, Opinion, Wit, and Advice from the 20th Century's Preeminent Writers*, the late African American writer James Baldwin said:

'Talent is insignificant. I know a lot of talented ruins. Beyond talent lie all the usual words: discipline, love, luck, but most of all, endurance.'

But my endurance tank was running dangerously low.

Barely a few days before my travels, I lost someone I thought I would spend the rest of my life with. For the very first time, I was in love, deeply, foolishly and recklessly. I astonished myself with my capacity to love so beautifully and infinitely. My love for him blazed with the warmth of an internal, eternal sun, which rose each time I saw his face, and set whenever we parted.

But his love was eclipsed by his ambition. Though the two of us were insatiably ambitious, in his own words, his work was his life. As I scrambled to keep the relationship afloat by over-compensating, I lost myself in furiously trying to fulfil his countless needs, and in proving that I was deserving of his love. The proud woman who would rely on no man metamorphosed into a mannequin to be picked up and put down when it suited him.

My Pashtun pride puffed its chest out, and my hyper-independence proudly insisted that I did not need *that much attention*. But waiting on the edge of a cliff for him to prioritise us gnawed at me excruciatingly slowly. As he lifted the bar higher and higher, in the same way I'd convinced myself that my inability to secure a full-time job was entirely my own fault, the fool in love that I was, I naively leapt over his hurdles unquestioningly, because surely, all the deficiencies lay with me.

Gradually the light of that internal sun began to diminish. I simply could not compete with glistening professional achievements and glowing words from those with power that were so important to him. The news of the lump brought a death sentence with it, but not the one you might expect: it was the crippling realisation that his needs would always come first, and that his ambition would always come before the relationship. And so I left.

I had built an Other London for him, where he and I could walk together hand in hand, untroubled and unhindered by the chaos of its twin, the real London, where the smog of car fumes and the sound of shuffling crowds numbed by the chaos of busyness gnawed like rats scuttling among the trash. I built the roads, paved the streets, erected the minarets of its mosques, painstakingly assembled the stained-glass windows of its churches, synagogues and temples.

I spilled the warmth of our love into its steamy coffee shops, the leafy sanctuary of the plane trees arching over the public gardens as a monument to us, to the roots we were supposed to plant together. Every fragment of London was a fragment of him.

But how could I grieve for him, who was dead in my memories? How could I wrap him in his burial shroud, mourn his memory, which lingered like the stubborn, sweet scent of fried onions, which refused to remove itself from my hair when my landlady prepared the day's dinner early in the morning?

Lost and alone, I became a ghost wandering through an unfamiliar city, a stranger in my own home. But, if like Audre Lorde, I am to write my own 'Litany for Survival' – because survive I must and survive I will – I must erase our footprints imprinted into the grey concrete, rename the streets, reclaim this home that I built for the both of us. I must chart out a new path for myself without him. When whispers of his memory reach me, cripple me with grief in the moments his face and the sound of his voice pass through me like heavy clouds of rain, I will not hide from them. I will grieve for his memory, burn it to ashes and blow them into the night sky to sit among the stars, a eulogy of light and darkness.

I built this London for the both of us. I buried him and mourned his memory in that Other London. And now I must build London anew, only this time, I will build it for myself.

إِنَّا لِلَّهِ وَإِنَّا اِلَيْهِ رَاجِعُونَ

Verily to God we belong, and to God we return

For most of my adult life, I have been running from vulnerability. Growing up in a single-mother household, I proudly learned to become self-reliant very early on. I always wore stoicism and my ability not to rely on others as a badge of honour. I shouldered the burdens of my past and present like the Greek god Atlas, who carried the earth on his shoulders. To be vulnerable was to be weak. To be weak was to be a burden.

I ducked and dived for as long as I could, convincing myself it would be too painful to walk through the fire, whether that fire was trying something and failing at it, risking my heart in allowing someone in, or my uncertainty over the future. I became hostage to my fears for so long, I began living with my eyes closed. My partner too demanded vulnerability from me. But the more I gave, convinced of my own deficiency, the more I became depleted, exhausted and resentful, and the more he retreated, floating out to sea on a ship I couldn't board, as if overwhelmed and disgusted by my uncontrollable weakness.

I was grieving, not just for someone I had loved and lost, or an elusive career title, but for the girl I used to be. The child within me would never have even imagined risking her heart in the way I had done. She is still there, hiding behind the brown of my eyes, quaking with fear. Only this time my older, fuller self has placed a firm hand on her heart, reassuring her: 'You will get through this storm just as you have with all the others.'

By running from vulnerability in all her guises, love, fear of the past, present and future, I became blind to the real truth: that even in my self-perceived 'brokenness', I am whole. And if that wholeness is shattered, then I must build a new wholeness from the shards left behind. I dared to love someone, and he lost me. I dared to dream and write an existence nobody had lived in the generations that came before me. I sought 'wholeness' within myself by loving another human being and anchoring my self-esteem to my career. I succeeded greatly and I failed even more spectacularly. Everything I feared in allowing myself to become vulnerable came to pass. But I am still standing. I am still breathing.

The Blue Mountain Peak is the highest point in Jamaica, towering 7,402 feet above sea level. Spanish colonists were evicted by the English, who ravenously seized the sugar gold mine of Jamaica for themselves in 1655. In the verdant mountainside of the Blue Mountain, former slaves, the

Maroons of African descent and indigenous Caribbean Taíno, revolted against their captors and found sanctuary there. Three hundred and sixty-five years later, I made an entirely different journey to find sanctuary in the summit and watch the sun rise.

Up Jacob's Ladder we trudged, a notoriously steep slope of dense fern trees and undergrowth blanketed in mist. There was no guide to lead us in the heavy darkness, just the burning orange lights of Kingston flickering thousands of feet below, spread out like an angel unfurling its wings, a lopsided crescent moon grinning at me as it floated in a carpet of stars, and the light from my iPhone casting a luminous path in front of me.

After five hours of hiking, with fresh bread pudding generously wrapped in cellophane by Zanifa, a Trinidadian aunty I met the day before, and some crushed cashew nuts from London, we reached the summit. Heartbroken, burned out, and awaiting the test results of the mystery lump, I found myself at the crosshairs of the unholiest of unholy trinities. If I just let the sunlight of the breaking dawn swallow me with its golden light, maybe the flotsam of thoughts knocking about in my head would disappear. Prayers whispered on a mountain-top would reach God quicker, I hoped, floating from Jamaica to the place where all prayers and dark thoughts uttered on summits swarm in clouds of melancholy and hope to comfort each other.

Vulnerability, I'd learned in the most painful way, is not some kind of pathology we need to shed in a reptilian manner. It is a crown of compassion that empowers us to extend an understanding for the grief of others, and to ourselves most of all. To love another person is one of the bravest things a human being can do. But more than that, to love yourself, to be at peace with yourself, is the bravest and most necessary act of all. The real prize was never to land the dream job or the man I thought would become my husband. It was a painful but necessary path to finding myself.

Brexit has plunged us deep into the 'Rivers of Blood' the Tory politician Enoch Powell lamented, and down a rabbit hole of populism, racism, Islamophobia. Covid-19 and the renewed spotlight on institutional racism in 'post-racial' America and its colonial parent, 'Great' Britain, has hammered home the reality that storytelling has never been more vital.

Even in the midst of heartbreak, the health scare, which thankfully turned out to be nothing at all, and my existential crisis, the last year only reinforced why I wanted to become a writer in the first place, and I'm grateful for it. I'm grateful for the highs that have led me to where I am, for the lessons failure can teach us when things don't go to plan or, like me, you set impossibly high standards for yourself only to collapse under the weight of it all. There *is* power in our voices. There *is* power in our stories. But the bitter truth is, if we don't write it or give life to it, if we don't push on and replenish the resilience engines Baldwin spoke of, then no one will.

Through storytelling, we can expand ideas of what it means to be British. As the poet Suhaiymah Manzoor-Khan says, 'Britain is Bismillah, Britain is Basmati rice.' All that, and everything else in between. For all the pain and baggage of the past, the anxiety over things that have and haven't come to pass, for the first time, I am living the complexity of a messier, fuller life – only this time, I'm no longer blindsided by a belief in my own deficiency. My eyes are finally wide open. ☾

THE BALLAD OF THE KANGAROO BANDIT
JOE ZADEH

From the summer of 1999, southern California was plagued by one of the most prolific bank robbers in American history. The man worked alone and moved strategically from city to city, bank to bank. By March of 2001, the FBI suspected he'd hit twenty-four banks in nineteen months. Sometimes he robbed two or three in a week. The media dubbed him the 'Kangaroo Bandit' because he wore a backpack on his chest – but I think they should have called him the Octopus. He was declared the most wanted man in California, but nobody could catch the Kangaroo Bandit.

'It's tempting to liken him to smoke,' reported the *Los Angeles Times* at the height of his spree. 'He coils in and out of view, his presence an omen of danger. Then he evaporates into a sunlit afternoon, while those left behind wonder what it is they have just seen.'[1]

The FBI knew the Kangaroo Bandit was around twenty-five to thirty years old, around 6 ft tall and around 200 lbs. He usually wore long-sleeved shirts, dark sunglasses and a baseball cap. Sometimes he ran off; other times, he got into a red Toyota pickup or a black sports car. But the human behind those details, the gross physical facts of skin, hair and bone, remained a mystery. You see, the Kangaroo Bandit had a special power: nobody could decide how he looked.

Witnesses described him as everything from a dark-skinned white male to a light-skinned African American. Some said Puerto Rican. Others said Brazilian. A few swore he was Middle Eastern. And some of the bank tellers were convinced he was wearing dark mascara. 'You know they all can't be right,' said FBI Agent Joseph White.[2] Photos and security-camera footage didn't help. Sometimes his skin looked fair, sometimes it looked dark. Sometimes he had a moustache, sometimes a beard, and sometimes he was completely clean-shaven. The Kangaroo Bandit was large, he contained multitudes.

The FBI asked the public for help, offering a $15,000 reward for anyone who could help them find the robber. Hundreds of people called in, turning in innocent men of every skin colour imaginable. Race is one of the fundamental ways society categorises people, and yet something was short-circuiting. He wasn't just moving between races, he was playing with them. The British–Jamaican sociologist Stuart Hall said that the body is a text, which we all inspect like literary critics – and yet nobody could read this man.[3]

I am no bank robber, but I have been likened to smoke. I was born in Gateshead and I am a mixed-race male – a Brown father (Iranian) and a white mother (English). Most people visually identify me as white: an Englishman with a Geordie accent and a decent tan. The same way they would have identified Steve Jobs as white, despite the fact his birth father was a Syrian Muslim from Homs called Abdulfattah Al-Jandali. And yet, just like the Kangaroo Bandit, my skin seems to change all the time.

The first time I was racially abused I was called a 'paki'. The second time I was called a 'dirty Israeli'. A Scottish girl once called me a 'fucking geranium', but that was just funny. I've had white people tell me I'm Brown, white people tell me

I'm white, Brown people tell me I'm white, and Brown people tell me I'm Brown. Iranians just tell me I'm not Iranian enough.

When I first went on a video call with the editors of this book, I irrationally convinced myself that they might see my face for the first time on camera and think, 'Oh, you're a lot whiter than we imagined. Sorry, we can't include you!'

People aren't what we wish them to be, nor what they seem to be. They are what they are. I am English. I am Iranian. I am geranium. I coil in and out of view. And while I may not evaporate into sunlit afternoons, my presence, especially in airports, is seen as an omen of danger.

Airports are the gladiatorial arena of race and ethnicity. Since the age of twenty-five, I've been taken to one side for an extra bag check or additional questions at almost every one I've visited, even on the small Channel Island of Guernsey, with its one runway. Yes, it's me. I have come to bomb the place where you make the gold top milk.

In 2019 I flew to New York. My bag was checked twice at security. Then, at the gates, I was taken to one side and put in a cordoned-off area with six other men; I was the only one who seemed visibly white. Two of them looked at me, perplexed. 'Iranian,' I said, and they smiled and went back to their phones.

Our bags were opened and checked. I boarded the plane, sat down and put on my seatbelt. Then my name was called over the tannoy, with a few others. My bags were removed from the overhead compartments and checked one more time, in front of the entire plane carriage. It was brutal and embarrassing. Yet I can't deny that somewhere deep inside me there was a strange sense of pride. At that moment I was more Iranian than ever.

Mixed-race people are often used to symbolise racial harmony, especially in advertising, where brands are keen to appear forward-thinking and inclusive. But my mixed-race experience has more often been one of inner conflict and confusion. In a world riven by racial fault lines, it's bewildering to exist in a rupture. To get by, you need to embrace contradiction, accept the mangle, and live in a state of cognitive dissonance, whereby the mind is always filled with conflicting thoughts and feelings. Split at the root. Racially ambiguous. Racially amphibious.

'I stand at the edge where earth touches ocean,' wrote the American–Mexican writer and self-described 'Chicana, *tejana*, working-class, dyke-feminist poet' Gloria E. Anzaldúa, 'where the two overlap / a gentle coming together / at other times and places a violent clash'.[4]

My English grandad was a lorry driver from a small village in Northumberland who fought for Churchill in World War Two, voted for Margaret Thatcher and always donated to 'the Legion'.[5] My Iranian grandad was a sugar maker from Tehran, and a card-carrying member of the Communist Party (known as the 'Tudeh' party). He despised Britain for the way it had invaded Iran in 1941, decimated his country and helped topple its democratic leaders during the 1953 Iranian coup d'état. My father often tells me, through humble laughter, that it's good he never lived to meet his British grandchildren, because he would have been ashamed to know they existed. At school, my father was taught how the evil British businessman William Knox D'Arcy stole Iran's oil, while my mother was taught how Britannia ruled the waves.

My English grandad was a good, kind man with big, bony hands and twinkling eyes, and the limited racial awareness quite typical of a small village in 1970s rural England. When my mother took my father to the village, Grandad took him to the local pub. The bar and lounge fell silent and nobody made eye contact. The village, at the time, had a population of around 1,500. Some, I'm told, had never seen a Brown man until my father walked in.[6] Grandad told my mother, 'He's nice, but I don't want you marrying a dark-skinned fella.'

My mother and father got married in 1983 anyway. Grandad and my father became good friends. They travelled to lorry shows together: shows where you look at lorries. They carried on going to the village pub, where Grandad would proudly announce him as 'my son-in-law'.

When my mixed-race forearms go their brownest, they don't remind me of my father, they remind me of Grandad. There was a certain milky paleness beneath my father's Iranian skin, but Grandad's English skin always turned a deep and musty olive after long afternoons tending the tomatoes in his greenhouse with his cream shirt sleeves rolled past the elbow. After a hot summer, his skin went slightly darker, even, than my Iranian father's. And yet this metaphysical concept floated in the air between them, still through friendship. A subtle difference invisible to the naked eye. Grandad's whiteness, my father's darkness.

A researcher in the Pacific coral reef once recorded seeing an octopus change colour 177 times in a single hour.[7] Yellow, red, brown, black, as well as glittering greens, blues, golds and pinks. Their colour can change with their mood, but more often than not, an octopus is trying to convince either predators or prey that it is really something else.

I did this on a cold doorstep in Telford, Shropshire, last winter. I was canvassing for the Labour Party ahead of the 2019 UK general election, speaking to a woman in her late forties outside her home. We were discussing everything from education to austerity; then she unleashed a long rant on immigration.

'How can we be paying all those taxes, and working so hard,' she said, 'and then we're put in a queue for the NHS behind all these unemployed immigrants?'

She didn't know I was the son of an immigrant. I imagine she assumed I would have been browner or blacker. She couldn't see the glittering greens, blues, golds and pinks. I felt desperate to tell her, but another part of me just wanted to listen. Unaware of where I came from, she voiced her prejudices freely – not defiant, almost confessional. In that moment, I was granted a view beyond the ugly weeds of her racism to see the roots below.

Once we moved past the fictional hordes of immigrants clogging up the hospitals and raking in benefits, it was clear she was wracked with genuine fears around health and financial insecurity. Her husband, who was self-employed, had become ill and been forced to take six months off work, in pain and not earning. Hearing his name, he joined us at the door on crutches. Life was quite visibly shit. But in the desperate search for blame, they'd taken a wrong turn. They didn't blame the government, who had just drastically downgraded their local hospital and closed the A&E. They missed the facts and found a scapegoat.

'Who's that lady we like, the one who tells it like it is?' she said.

I took a few hopeful guesses.

'Katie Hopkins,' said her husband.

I realise that to some, to just stand and listen would have been inconceivable. My father would have found it inconceivable. But part of the white privilege I carry is that racism is not a part of my everyday life. It's rare and quick, not everywhere and always. In a way, I felt white enough to entertain her. With my identity cloaked, I got a little look at the conditions in which her racism grew.

The Filipino-American clinical psychologist Maria P. P. Root has argued that mixed-race individuals can expand the discussion and potentially take us beyond race.[8] After all, we have both feet in both groups. And in a world of maddening polarisation – in which people seem stuck in alternate realities, where each side has their own facts, histories, and narratives – I can see the powerful role of someone who has experienced both white privilege and racism. We're like walking sociological experiments, wooden horses rolling through the gates of Troy.

And yet, I couldn't bring myself to say anything much at all to this woman and her husband. The moment was there and I just watched with wide eyes. What do I say? How do I say it? And why me? Who do I think I am? Some sort of mixed-race messiah? I made a few half-hearted points and shrugged at things I didn't agree with, then fake-smiled a goodbye and walked away. In the shower, for weeks afterwards, I replayed the scenario in my head in a thousand different ways.

The village church wouldn't allow my father, a Brown non-Christian, to be married there, so my parents did the ceremony at Newcastle Civic Centre and then, in a charming act of defiance, drove to the village church afterwards and took their photos outside. A passer-by who went to school with my mother walked over to congratulate her. When she pointed out my father as her husband, he sighed and said, 'Could you not have found a nice English bloke?'

I used to think their interracial wedding photos seemed so radical and groundbreaking for eighties northern England. But then I did some reading and found out there were married interracial couples living in Newcastle as far back as the second century (like Regina of St Albans and Barates of Palmyra, now modern Syria, who lived together in North Shields, a small town on the north bank of the River Tyne). The Cambridge classicist Mary Beard cited them, and many other examples, in a debate sparked in 2017 when the alt-right conspiracy theorist Paul Joseph Watson wrote that a BBC programme depicting a mixed-race family in Ancient Britain was 'the Left' trying to 'rewrite history'.

When you know about Regina and Barates – and the racial mixing that has always under-pinned British history, from Chinese communities in nineteenth-century Liverpool to the Arab, West African and Caribbean communities of Cardiff's Tiger Bay that pre-date the Windrush Generation of 1948 – it's hard to swallow the various books, news stories and academic papers that come out every year beckoning the approaching future of 'mixed-race Britain' – like this is a novel moment for civilisation. The growing population of 'mixed-race' Britain would be better described as a growing population of people whose race has mixed in living memory. Even using the term 'mixed race' sometimes feels, to me, like accepting the notion that racial purity does exist, somewhere out there.

How do we measure racial purity? Where are the boundaries of my whiteness and brownness?

If I have a child with a fellow mixed-race person, are they mixed-race? If I have a child with a white person, will they be half mixed-race? Or will they just be white? Where is the cut-off point? Where does the ocean touch the earth? And who decides this? When will my mixedness be flushed out of the system? Can you be a third-generation immigrant? Fourth? How much of your racial identity is what you are and how much of it is what people see in you?

When we talk about our genealogy, why do we only go back so far? Genetic testing has repeatedly shown that Europe is a melting pot of bloodlines from Africa, the Middle East and the Russian steppe. The geneticist Adam Rutherford estimated that over 500 years, each of us has around 1,048,576 ancestors.[9] Inside us all there bubble ancient cocktails that have been shaken since the very beginning. Your blood is probably as mixed as mine; I was just mixed recently.

Sometimes I like to watch YouTube 'reaction videos' of people doing 23andMe tests and discovering that they are 15 per cent African, or 10 per cent Native American, or 5 per cent Jewish, or all three. And yet there is something in their voices that makes me think they just can't comprehend it. 'Either we are all multiracial, or, really, none of us are,' said the Filipino-American philosopher Ronald Sundstrom.[10] Or, as Andy Warhol – the late Slovak-American artist and son of two working-class Lemko emigrants, a distinct minority ethnic group from the Lemkivshchyna region of Eastern Europe – quite decadently put it, 'If everybody's not a beauty, then nobody is.'[11]

The FBI never caught the Kangaroo Bandit. After he'd robbed over one hundred banks, he simply handed himself in, having come to the conclusion that his crimes were not as 'victimless' as he first thought. And when he was finally identified and imprisoned, the trick of his baffling invisibility was revealed. The Kangaroo Bandit was neither Black, white, Puerto Rican, Brazilian or Middle Eastern. You already know why. A Black father and a white mother had created a man who looked like almost everything in between. ☾

SHELTER IN PLACE
SANJANA VARGHESE

When the Covid-19 pandemic set in, much of what we'd call regular life transformed rapidly. The UK government abandoned the widely criticised 'herd immunity' plan (in which as many people as possible get ill) and U-turned. Suddenly, it was paramount that everyone who could stay home did so for as long as possible. Overnight, the public and private spheres collapsed into each other, without any warning. Every time I try to describe it, I think about those *Tasty* videos of spherical desserts – something hot and liquid is poured on top of the chocolate ball, and eventually it caves in.[1] It mixes together and melts, and you're left with something you can't separate.

As a freelance journalist, I was used to the idea that there was no delineation between the place where I worked and the place where I slept, but I found a strange fog settling over my daily routine, like everything I needed or wanted to do was doused in treacle. For the *New Yorker*, Jamaica Kincaid once wrote: 'A house has a physical definition; a home has a spiritual one.' Home became more than just a location – it also became the axis around which everything else turned.[2]

I set out to write an essay on public space, something which I thought would touch on immigrant communities and ethnic minorities, psychogeography, gentrification and redlining, the processes by which public and private space are given over to profit and productivity. I didn't anticipate that we would be forced indoors, and I did not realise that much of what I was thinking about would be turned on its head.

Since I moved to London six years ago, I have moved every year. The flat that I am locked down in, where I have lived for a year and a half, is the place that I've actually felt most at home. It's very narrow – we can just about fit a bike in the reception hallway – but my room has a big window and space for a desk. I know I am lucky: I live in between two beautiful parks and near supermarkets, with a friend and two other flatmates who I like. The back of my flat is the roof of a shop, and we put tables and chairs out there and drink when it's warm. I've waved to my neighbours more in the last two months than I have ever before, and for brief glimpses, I've even forgotten that these specific changes are a necessity rather than a choice.

Space itself has always been political. Henri Lefebvre, a Marxist philosopher, wrote about the relationship between physical space and capitalism, the idea that space itself was not just a place that needed to be filled with people, but that our social relations were often structured and changed because of our built environment.[3]

I am increasingly finding it hard to believe that more of the world exists outside of the radius of what I can walk to in forty minutes. I spend more time online than I normally do – because there's nothing else to do, and because that's where my life is now. I've started to spend hours on *Architectural Digest* videos, looking at wealthy people's houses. The other day, I saw an acquaintance on the other side of Clissold Park, a park in north London near where I live, and it felt like a splash of cold water to the face as we waved at each other. I scroll back through my camera roll and wince when I see something that feels unachievable

– like a photo of a group of friends at a pub garden, or a screenshot of a cinema ticket in the middle of the day. I can't reproduce social intimacy online, through a screen, because it feels like a weak imitation of the real thing.

The concept of public space has completely changed and collapsed in on itself. You use the same screen and software to call people for work (albeit not the case for essential workers), and to call your friends. Elements of your life brush up against each other in now predictable ways. It places your friends and co-workers and other people who you've never met – like an artist doing a webinar, or a DJ on Instagram Live – all in the same frame of reference, and flattens them. The unreal feels as close as the everyday, and the idea of a 'public' exists almost completely on the internet.

Often, public space has been a contested site. Networks of surveillance, a CCTV camera on every corner and private security guards have proliferated in massive cities around the world, increasingly sold as a trade-off for living in a metropolis. But the exemption of the private sphere from capital P politics is, in itself, political.

Feminist and disability scholars would argue that relationships and dynamics outside of the home are often replicated at home too (and vice versa). For marginalised communities, taking up space is seen as a progression rather than a negation. So, a worldwide crisis which requires staying at home, away from the public eye, to protect other people, goes against our most basic instincts. What we are living through – where public space is now a site of danger, and everything else has shifted online – does feel intensely unfamiliar for some.

What has been immediately telling is the language of staying at home, a case study in psychogeography writ large. In the United States, governors issued 'shelter-in-place' orders, reminiscent of a catastrophic event – wherever you are, hunker down and make it your home. The use of the word 'shelter' implies a temporary state of affairs, like everything will be over in a few weeks. In the United Kingdom, the Conservatives went for a three-pronged approach: 'stay home, save lives, protect the NHS'. Home, in this view, is a fixed location – a place where you can hunker down and isolate from the rest of the world, somewhere safe and stable. Homeless people were temporarily housed in hotels, only to find that they would be forced to leave once it was no longer strictly necessary for them to be taken care of. Little was done for people for whom home is neither a fixed location nor a place of safety.

During the first month of lockdown, when we were still navigating the boundaries of what was acceptable and what wasn't, every weekend felt like Groundhog Day. The days had mixed together, like wading through sand away from the tide. I watched as official police Twitter accounts posted photos of people in parks – for the most part, social distancing responsibly – and admonished people for being out of their houses. Columnists and people with backyards would then pile on, asking whether it really was so hard to avoid going to the park. Then came a cycle of outrage – how can people be expected to avoid parks if housing is so poorly ventilated, so cramped? – and then the police would threaten to shut down parks, and the cycle would repeat.

But the logic of private space – a radius of two metres around us, one that no one can transgress – is one that we now have to carry with us.

'Walking too close to someone can become almost immoral, regardless of whether the streets are too narrow to socially distance.' If someone walks close to you, it becomes almost immoral, regardless of whether the streets are too narrow to socially distance. As the days wear on, I notice marks on the ground outside stores and shops. Some of them are chalk, and others are marking tape, and eventually they become all I can see anywhere. When I walk by somewhere with an open door, I find my eyes drawn downward, trying to figure out how obtrusive I find these markers of physical distance, a reminder to stay away from each other. It's gotten to the point where I cast my eyes downward near my own door, looking for that telltale white line. Benjamin Bratton of the Strelka Institute wrote that this state of affairs created 'paranoid new relations' between the outside and the inside, a fear of what lies out there – a feeling that I hate to admit has settled into me.[4]

The Tory government has continuously individualised responsibility for the pandemic.[5] If you aren't classified as an essential worker, but your boss is still making you come into work, the responsibility is yours alone. If your livelihood depended on you leaving the house, the responsibility was yours alone – even if your boss was making you come in. If you were laid off, but hadn't managed to save up, that was because you, an individual, had failed to adequately prepare for a global pandemic. The five-week wait for Universal Credit wasn't shortened, either. If people were out of their homes – if they were sunbathing, or they were buying 'non-essential' items, or they weren't socially distancing – they were abdicating a civic duty. It was a dereliction of some kind of patriotism.

Not leaving the house unless you had to morphed into a matter of patriotism. If you could work from home, have food brought to you and run around in your backyard, you were one of the people who was doing the most for your country.

The message was clear – the world should have shrunk for most people. It should be composed of the four walls you live in, with a green space or a supermarket thrown in for good measure. For many people, this isn't the case. Essential workers, such as nurses, cleaners, supermarket employees, doctors, waste collectors, and others, are now visibly keeping society running, shouldering the burden of the pandemic, on the front lines against a disease which had been mismanaged at every step. Since the beginning of the pandemic, the UK has had the dubious honour of having the highest death toll in the world, eventually being over-taken by the US.

It has been impossible to ignore the racialised element to this pandemic. The official Public Health England review[6] states that Black and Asian ethnic groups are disproportionately at risk from Covid-19 compared to their white counter-parts, and the precarious workforce currently keeping societies running is disproportionately made up of ethnic minorities.[7]

When it comes to secure housing, stable employ-ment, access to green space and all the other factors which would make isolation easier to bear, ethnic minorities are once more disadvantaged at every turn. They make up over half of the overcrowded households in Britain, have up to eleven times less green space to access[8] and are twice as likely to be unemployed.[9] Ethnic minorities are much less likely to be living in a stable housing situation, let alone to own their own house.[10]

As life moves online, those groups of people who are left behind in the flesh-and-blood world are left behind online too. When the Labour Party proposed an 'internet for all' policy in 2019, it was denounced as broadband communism. But it should be obvious that the answer to the question of who has access to the internet is the determinant of who can access the rest of society itself. Physical locations themselves are not immune to this move online.

I've begun to think about some of the places I went to often, such as Ridley Road Market in Dalston, east London, which has existed for over sixty years – it's always busy, full of stalls and sellers, people moving in and out with bags full of shopping. Even after new residential buildings sprang up overnight, the market has held its place. It smells of fish even on the weekends, long after the market packs up, and it's a crucial part of the neighbourhood, which has always been home to many immigrant and migrant communities. Over 10 per cent of the neighbourhood is Black or Black Caribbean,[11] and Hackney even has its own Carnival, ten days after Notting Hill's Carnival events. And yet during this pandemic, a group of housing developers held a Zoom meeting to discuss going ahead with plans to demolish it and regenerate the area, to make it into something sterile. No one from the local community was asked to dial in.

In an edition of her monthly newsletter about sickness, the writer and poet Anne Boyer writes that 'fear educates our care for each other – we fear a sick person might be made sicker, or that a poor person's life might be made even more miserable, and we do whatever we can to protect them because we fear a version of human life in which everyone lives only for themselves'.[12] That seems like a reorientation of Bratton's 'paranoid relations', a new way of reconfiguring fear as a driving force. I watched and joined in as mutual aid networks popped up around me in every direction, with strangers caring for each other in the absence of a larger directive to do so. I have bitten my tongue while public figures who have built their careers on justifying the devastation of vulnerable communities have gone on TV every night to talk about how important Britain's precarious workforce is.

I am tired of couching the value of people's lives in productivity, like these people didn't matter before they were disinfecting hospital surfaces or taking people's garbage away. During this period of lockdown, I've watched as the days tick by and wondered whether anything would be done for the immigrants, asylum seekers and migrants who currently live in the UK. Parts of the justice system are effectively frozen, and people are still in detention at centres like Yarl's Wood, where the only crime that anyone has committed is daring to want a better life for themselves.

In the *New Yorker*, Kim Stanley Robinson writes about how this pandemic has reshaped what we think of as the future: 'It's a new feeling, this alienation and solidarity at once. It's the reality of the social; it's seeing the tangible existence of a society of strangers, all of whom depend on one another to survive.'[13] He suggests that we may emerge with a new 'structure of feeling', where we value the right things, and keep on valuing them. What seems fundamental now – community, protecting the vulnerable, putting each other above ourselves – may be cast as less so in the coming months, especially if politicians believe that the time for care has passed.

In a 2013 essay called 'Joy', the novelist Zadie Smith states: 'Perhaps the first thing to say is that I experience at least a little pleasure every day.'[14] She describes the simple pleasures that are also my favourite parts of living in a city – seeing unfamiliar faces, describing them to the people you love, long walks, strange encounters. Those elements of everyday life feel like a distant memory, but I'm trying to reconfigure my thinking. Perhaps those parts of public life may not return for some time, and maybe when they do return, it will be part and parcel of a new kind of world.

Many people seem to be saying that post-pandemic, society will be fundamentally altered for the better. In reality, no one knows what the world will look like after this pandemic, if there even is a clear, delineated 'after' point. Lefebvre wrote often about the fact that everyday life, the monotony and dullness of it, is necessary to keep capitalism functioning as normal. I hope that that normal is gone, even if my most cynical instincts tell me that it's only been more deeply entrenched.

But I will continue to hold Anne Boyer's words in my head daily – 'fear educates our care for each other'. It means thinking about the value of fear as love in the broadest sense, which is something closer to solidarity. ☾

THE SHALLOWS
NASRI ATALLAH

I was twenty-five the first time I realised I didn't
know how to breathe. Sitting on a bench in central London's Soho Square, the sun was cold as it
wrapped itself around the lunchtime office workers pouring in from the nearby production houses
and record labels to bite into their midday sand-
wiches. The high-visibility vests of two construc-
tion workers sitting at the opposite end of the
park caught the light and slung it across a cluster
of pigeons congregated on the fraying grass. I
started to take in a breath, as if to inhale the
scene, to keep this moment inside me. But the
breath snagged on something in my sternum. I let
out a series of sharp, shallow breaths. This isn't
how people breathe, I thought.

My laboured breathing presented itself again in
the middle of a hike in Norway. It was Christmas
and we were visiting my brother-in-law on the
edges of Oslo. The park near his home extends

into a hiking trail that is everything you imagine Nordic perfection to be: frozen lakes, dense, dark greenery, lush woodland, and extremely fit people breezing past. Wheezing, the shards of frozen air cutting at my throat, I made a note to call the doctor on my return to London. It had been ten years; it was time to ask someone about this.

The sterile environment of the clinic was punctuated by National Health Service (NHS) messages about mindfulness, alcoholism and ways to stop smoking. My name flashed up on a screen. For a moment, its Arabness floating in the middle of the waiting room made me uncomfortable.

I explained to the doctor about Norway, about the bench in Soho Square, about a million other instances where my body had acted against me. She told me that the answers lie in a spirometry test, meant to assess how well my lungs are working by measuring how much air I can inhale and exhale – and how quickly I can do it.

The nurse was kind in the way every nurse in the NHS is kind, and I embarked on a set of breathing exercises. Wrapping my lips around the plastic measuring device, and puffing my cheeks like a talentless jazz trumpeter. My breathing was medically normal, she told me, somewhat sadly. The problem must lie elsewhere.

'Where do you breathe from?' she asked.

It was a question no one had ever asked me.

After a moment of confusion, I pressed my index finger into a point in the middle of my chest. The nurse looked at me with a mix of satisfaction and pity. She placed all of her fingers against her stomach and pushed inward, as if to knead. She simulated a deep, performative breath, saying, 'It should come from here.' Strengthen your core, and you'll be fine. The knowledge that the source of my breathing problems was solvable was of some comfort, though strengthening my core wasn't exactly on my immediate to-do list.

One place I breathe well is sinking into a replica mid-century armchair in the low light of a therapy session. As the words fall out of me, tumbling across the windowless room towards my therapist, I feel like an eavesdropper taking in someone else's epiphanies. I breathe in the moments where I forget myself, in the effortlessness of coaxed self-realisation. Over the course of therapy, I have understood things I didn't know I was supposed to understand.

One of them was debunking the unsubstantiated suspicion I always held that the apartments on Airbnb are full of cameras and listening devices. I had never articulated this paranoid thought while planning holidays, because it felt like the kind of thing you say before your friends politely nod and back away from you. Over the course of fifty minutes, I realised that the roots of that paranoia were planted somewhere different.

My whole life, I considered my dual British–Lebanese identity to have impacted only trivial things, like what television shows to watch or foods to like. It was responsible for embarrassment at my accented English and my rickety Arabic. It turned out that in their scuffle within me, my rival identities had formed the shape of my feelings about privacy and security.

I moved from London to Beirut for the first time at the age of fourteen. One of the things that changed the most for me was the sudden impression of being constantly under surveillance. The tentacles of the intelligence services reached into the landlines – they were, I felt sure, listening in on conversations in the intimacy of people's homes. Meanwhile, strangers-turned-informants made every interaction with someone a new source of possible incrimination.

The 'sharing economy', as it has been euphemistically called, was incompatible with the suspicions baked into me by those years.

Through therapy it became clear my identities had decided what rooms I felt safe in. Was my identity also dictating when I might be allowed to breathe?

In her 2019 essay collection *Trick Mirror*, Jia Tolentino writes, 'I've been thinking about five intersecting problems: first, how the internet is built to distend our sense of identity; second, how it encourages us to overvalue our opinions; third, how it maximizes our sense of opposition; fourth, how it cheapens our understanding of solidarity; and, finally, how it destroys our sense of scale.'

Over the years I had mediated many of my thoughts through Facebook. It was the only way an idea could exist. A version of therapy. Then a fissure emerged and I started to slip away from the platform.

When the Cambridge Analytica scandal erupted into the news, outlining the political consultancy's misuse of Facebook users' data, the underlying knowledge that I was complicit in my own surveillance was impossible to ignore. I took part in an inventory of my digital life. I deleted old Facebook posts and tweets the way you would unceremoniously throw out old receipts. I came to the realisation that a new form of therapy would be a safer bet than crowdsourced angst relief.

Years earlier, in Lebanon, I had engaged in my first attempts at therapy, which had largely failed. I always resorted to it in moments of crisis: an angry outburst or a near breakdown. The conversations had been conducted in a mix of French and Lebanese Arabic. But I am not myself in either of those languages. I am versions of myself, I suppose. But not the versions that make meaningful decisions about life.

For my first attempt at therapy after moving back to London, I started in a very different place. I joined a series of six group-therapy sessions provided by the NHS. They took place in a multipurpose room at St Pancras Hospital in north London. The linoleum of the corridor squeaked under my feet as I moved towards the door to enter my first session. The hallway was lined with a row of small gouache portraits, some framed, others askew, all haphazardly added to the wall as an afterthought with the help of adhesive putty; the kind of artwork that attempts, unsuccessfully, to make a place like this feel less grim.

At the end of the hour, the group was asked to write a fear about this therapeutic journey onto a brightly coloured Post-it note. Mine was hot pink. I scribbled something on it and placed it in an envelope we were to be given back in six weeks. It felt a bit craft-like, infantile. When the envelope returned a month and a half later, I had forgotten what was written on the note. Against the hot pink of the paper my words felt alien and immature: 'I hope getting better doesn't change me.'

At best, the group therapy was practical, but it hadn't unlocked anything in my chest. I had pages and pages of cognitive behavioural therapy tips and tricks at my disposal, the materials from the sessions, but my shoulders still slumped forward. It was time for something different, something more intimate.

I had avoided looking up private therapists since I had returned to London, marked by my failed experiences in Lebanon and imagining they would be prohibitively expensive. I eventually dragged myself to a website and found that, while a significant investment, the sessions were more affordable than they had been in Beirut.

Confused by the alphabet soup of acronyms under every prospective therapist's photo, I decided to pick one based on how friendly their face looked. As with most new relationships, I was only half-convinced. But by the end of the first session, I realised that speaking one-on-one with a therapist in English was going to be revolutionary.

I came in speaking as myself, not as a person mediated through the complicated neural entanglement of multilingualism. That 1.30 p.m. slot on Wednesdays became foundational, a vanishing point giving perspective to the rest of my week. Even in the weeks when I didn't have much to discuss, I still found myself excavating something, feeling lighter. Breathing.

In *Becoming Arab in London*, Dr Ramy Aly writes:

Mediated representations of Arabs in Britain build upon a long-standing tradition of

Orientalism that casts Arabs as having a primitive, violent and misogynistic culture (singular) and thus essence. The fetishisation of 'The Arabs' means that 'Arab' becomes synonymous with terrorist and petro-dollar 'exotics'. [...] It has been the burden of Arabs in London, from Dr Zada in 1933 to Dr Mehdi in the 1970s all the way through to those raised and living in London in the early twenty-first century like Fadwa, to object to that representation and to try and 'correct it'.[1]

The morning of the 2005 London bombings, where fifty-six people died and over 700 people were injured, I slept in and missed being on the Piccadilly Line. I could never wake up on time for work. I walked the rest of the way to Holborn, finding out what occurred when I passed an electronics shop. I stood there in the street looking at the screens of discounted television sets like an extra in an apocalyptic film. When I made it to the office, I received a round of applause.

A year later, around the anniversary of the bombings, I was in a West End club celebrating a friend's birthday. Someone on the dance floor heard us speaking in Arabic. He said something racist. There was drunk male posturing. I thought it was over until I got outside and they beat me to a pulp.

I had been terrified of moving back to London since I had left in 2009. My last experiences of it were miserable, working in a banking job that eroded and blunted me. I surrounded myself with an expanding group of alluring, troublesome people who couldn't have been much happier than I was. I moved back to London in 2016, a different person from the one who had left seven years earlier. I was now in the city with my wife, Nour, and a desire to start my life over. Those Wednesday therapy sessions, an hour at a time, became a big part of rebuilding my identity.

One of the things I insisted on was that we live far away from where I grew up in south-west London. We ended up in Kentish Town, a part of north-west London that has been gentrifying since the late nineties. We were further contributing to the gentrification: a designer and a writer moving into a cosy flat in a former Victorian denture factory. My mum would later tell me it was a funny place to pick, this part of north London, because she used to take my sister and me to the Queen's Crescent Market around the corner as children. It was where I'd bought fake Reebok Pumps in 1991, when she had estimated the real pair didn't fit in the family finances. I remembered the market but didn't realise it was the one five minutes from my new home.

Before we had moved together from Beirut, I promised Nour London was a multicultural oasis where all of our problems would be solved. We were leaving behind the dysfunction of power cuts, a trash crisis and endemic corruption for a life in the heart of Europe's most exciting capital. I told her I would be myself in London, a less angry and despondent version of the man I was in Lebanon. Then, a few months after we were settled in, the United Kingdom voted to leave the European Union.

My chest tightened at the news, like a clenched fist at the centre of who I thought I was. Europe, the whole continent, had always been the hyphen between the two sides of me, and I was suddenly split open, either part drooping away from the chasm in the centre. My first reaction was to plan our departure, to create distance between us and my broken promise. I felt suddenly unwelcome in the very place I had planned to settle.

Rooting myself was important now. Up until that point, I had lived my life with a half-packed suitcase as an ornament in the corner of the bedroom by the chest of drawers. While the British utopia I had expected peeled away, revealing what had always been there, I did find an Arabness within me that I hadn't been able to quite hold on to before. Uprooted from our homelands, in London we created a refuge with our friends that could not exist elsewhere. And this new self in London started to remind me of the home I lived in growing up. Again, in wanting something entirely new, I had somehow found myself back at the beginning.

My father, Samir, has been a writer for some of the leading Arab newspapers for over six decades. From the 1970s to the 1990s, London 'was central to the emergence of a pan-Arab daily press and the proliferation of transnational Arabic publications',[2] with various newspaper offices dotted around Holborn and west London. Our home became a space for these people from all around the Arab world to meet, eat vast meals of lamb and rice and lovingly rolled stuffed vine leaves, drink tar-black Arabic coffee spiced with cardamom and smoke cigarettes. Today, as I create my own version of London, so many of my friends in the city are Egyptian, Kuwaiti, Saudi, Palestinian, Jordanian, Lebanese, Syrian and Iraqi. Even those who aren't Arab turn out to be Greeks, Cypriots, Italians. Or Brits who grew up on the Mediterranean, or long for it.

At first it felt surprising, exclusionary almost. Until I realised how important my childhood had been in teaching me how to be three things: a Londoner, Arab and Mediterranean. Every year, my parents, my sister and I would pile into our car in west London and make the long drive down to Villeneuve-Loubet, a commune ten kilometres up the Côte D'Azur from Nice. My parents continued their day-to-day life from there for the whole three months of summer. My father wrote all summer on the balcony and faxed his articles to the paper, while my sister and I created summer lives for ourselves. We both remember it as a happy place. Instinctively we understood that it fulfilled a purpose that our home in London couldn't. Not because it was foreign, but because it felt so familiar. Even not knowing our parents' native Lebanon, seeing them comfortable there made us comfortable. Later, when I'd end up living in Beirut on and off for ten years, looking out at the horizon, it took me a while to understand I was looking at the same sea, however absurd that may sound.

I never thought about it much until a few years ago, when my father told me he had always wanted rootlessness for me. I never wanted to tell you what you were or where you were from, he said, so you could never have that place taken away from you, like it was taken away from us.

'I wanted you to belong nowhere,' he told me over dinner one night.

Growing up in the UK, being sent to a French school, being taught Arabic, spending long periods outside of London, all these were deliberate strategies to confuse me. Like the tangle of wires behind a television, my competing identities made sure something flickered on the screen, but it wasn't a pretty way to organise things.

By the time the Covid-19 pandemic spread

across the world in the first months of 2020, I had been in therapy for eighteen months. As we progressively peeled away from each other and reduced all the contact that makes us human, my Wednesday therapy sessions, like everything else, moved into the virtual ether. By that point, our one-bedroom flat had become home, office and refuge to my wife and I. I didn't want to add 'therapist's office' to the list of activities that needed to coexist in its square footage.

In a show of mercy, the parks were kept open during the lockdown. I decided to walk to a nearby park and sit on a bench for the first of these new phone sessions. It was immediately different, trying to relax while I watched joggers' impossible attempts to avoid each other by exactly the government-mandated distance. For the second session I changed parks. I found a smaller, unloved one. I preferred it there; there was less to look at.

As I settled into the call, my therapist told me she was quitting her practice. The next week would be our last conversation. She was apologetic, remorseful. I respected the boundaries of the relationship too much to ask what was happening. I contented myself with an almost whispered, 'Is everything OK?'

She told me that if I wanted to find another therapist, it was recommended that I wait around three months. Like a real breakup, I thought to myself.

I lasted a month and a half before I started looking again. It felt as if everything inside me had compacted into a ragged stone in the middle of my torso again. Again, I went through the tedious process of selecting a therapist. This time, it felt more casual, as if less was at stake. I looked for someone kind. A French name stood out. I nodded at the acronyms under the name, as if conducting a job interview with a web page.

As with everything during the Covid-19 pandemic, this new encounter would be happening from home. Strong wifi and the familiarity of the screens into which my whole life had migrated: cocktail parties with friends, work meetings, seminars about the future of my industry, yoga classes, and now the person who would be trying to help me feel better again. When I was offered a choice of weekdays for our first session, I chose Wednesday, 2 p.m. Close enough.

I clicked on the link and my face appeared on the screen. I angled the laptop to make sure my bookcase was visible. This call would not be spared the ornamentation necessary to a life lived on video conference. The therapist appeared on the screen, and I noticed a rip in the sofa behind her. She looked both soft and angular and spoke with the accented English of a French person who has been in London for at least a decade.

The conversation was awkward, as any first meeting should be. But then, as the unhelpful timer in the corner of the chat window indicated we were heading into our twentieth minute together, she paused and leaned in.

'Do you have problems breathing?' she asked.

I pulled back, caving in on myself, as if she had headbutted me through both of our wifi connections. How could someone feel my breathing through this flat, detached, unfeeling medium? It felt like a violation, almost.

In our next session I told her I felt vulnerable, embarrassed really, when she noticed my breathing over a video call.

'When was the last time you drew a full breath?' she asks.

My mind went blank for a minute. Then I saw my legs dangling over a concrete jetty, my toes making circles in the clear water.

'On the Mediterranean; I'm not sure where,' I said.

I closed my eyes for a moment, trying to make sense of my memories. I felt like I was organising files on a computer. All of the Mediterranean moments come together.

'What do you feel?' she asked.

I motioned downwards, my hands just exiting the video-conference frame. It felt like I was breathing, moving the car wreck in my chest into other parts of my body and eventually outward.

That's normal, she said – you grew up on the Mediterranean. I want to correct her; I think, *That isn't true*. My British brain has somehow categorised the Mediterranean as a glossy summer destination plastered on a billboard under a grey London sky; it has made the Mediterranean somewhere exotic, the place where the olives at supermarkets come from.

But in that moment, I remembered the time I

travelled to meet the Syrian poet Adunis. Often referred to as the 'greatest living Arab poet', Adunis left Syria for Beirut in 1956 before settling in Paris in 1985.³ I asked about his exile from Syria, as some have described it.

'There is no exile for me,' he said, in what would become a profile for *GQ Middle East*.⁴ 'A human being, as soon as he exits the womb, is exiled. Exile is a political word. The nation is where you live in freedom. It's not your father or mother or your tribe. That's why I don't feel exiled. I feel free here.' He pointed to his chest calmly and said, 'The only place I can be exiled is inside, if I am unable to express myself.'

Maybe I also carry this capacity to be myself wherever I happen to be physically. Those annual stays in Villeneuve-Loubet, and the view from home in Beirut: the Mediterranean is home, and it is within me. It is the connective tissue between my identities. Its tables are full of flavourful misshapen fruit and vegetables, its wines, its reckless driving, its vast families jostling at impromptu gatherings, its laid-back approach to, well, everything. From Lebanon to Tunisia, Egypt to Spain, Turkey to

Tunisia, Spain to Greece, the Mediterranean – this Middle Sea – feels mine suddenly. Suddenly, it is a place to breathe. ☾

THE ILLEGITIMATE INDIAN
CYRINE SINTI

My maternal nani – dark Brown, twinkle-eyed, with three gold hoops through her wide nose – stood next to my paternal oma: light white, dead-eyed with a shy blush in her thin lips. The two of them are so opposingly different that you wonder how these two women are linked.

My great-grandmother, Isha, was born in Punjab to Banjara Gypsies; her mother was a dancing Gypsy, and her father a Rajasthani crafts-man and singing Gypsy.

They danced, sang, created, loved and lived in their homeland before discrimination and violent incidents forced them *ando drom* – on the road.

Like so many Gypsies before them, hatred dragged them from their birthright, from the land of their ancestors, their history and the only place their dark skin and mother tongue fit. They left with their pride and with pieces of our culture immortalised. They moved through Europe and settled in Germany, sharing the gifts that had come intuitively to them. Dance, song, crafts and natural magic: the very things that are used to romanticise Gypsies.

We aren't seen as a community of wide-ranging people. We are seen as one large dance troupe, but some Gypsies don't dance for their dinner. They work in offices, schools, restaurants and hospitals. There are Gypsies who don't practise any form of magic whatsoever. There are Gypsies who detest me using the word 'Gypsy', preferring Romani instead. We're a vast group of varying opinions, lifestyles and behaviours.

My lifestyle – belly dancing and lying under full moons for my soul – is not because of my Gypsy heritage. It's a Sinti family tradition. My family's lifestyle – sex work and criminal records – has nothing to do with my Gypsy heritage. It's survival and defence, not an argument for forced Romani sterilisation.

One tie that unites us, however, is the Porajmos. The Devouring. The Holocaust.

My family thinned after the unholy slaughtering of Gypsy people. Isha and my nani left Auschwitz in body only. 'The smell and scars will cling to us for the next hundred lives, Cyrine,' my nani said. Isha's surviving siblings, unbeknownst to her, had made their way back to India over the years that followed, while she ended up in east Slovakia among fellow Gypsies.

There, she would raise her family, feeding and vehemently defending them, essentially creating a tribe of illiterate sex workers. Some may consider us sinners, but morals can't feed children in a land that still has signs saying 'No Gypsies' in public places.

We were Punjabi-Romanese-speaking Gypsies, and different from the ones we lived among in tongue, tradition and ties. We kept our link to India alive and well through our daily lives. How could we not?

We were classified SINTI upon the liberation of the concentration camps; our family name had been stripped alongside our dignity. Our skin remained Brown and our blood still sang Banjara folk songs decades later, when I was pushed into this world, hazy on the slivovica-and-vodka epidural Ma needed to help her.

Because medicine isn't for the Gypsies.

Dignity isn't for the Gypsies.

Children shouldn't be for the Gypsies.

Because those who can fix these injustices already know about them and are often, in fact, the perpetrators. So, we do what we always do: carry on surviving in the face of racial discrimination, segregation, right-wing violence and left-wing indifference. When our periods begin, so does our work. But in this squalor, I had my own little privilege.

I was half white.

I'm the oddly coloured thread holding Gypsy anarchy and German Aryanism together. Midnight moon rituals, sex work and ethnic defiance to my left, white supremacy, bare-knuckle fighting and fascist contempt to my right. Both met each other within me.

It's a reality I've always known. My blood consists of the worst stereotypical examples of each culture, but I embrace both.

I am a Gypsy. I am German. I am Cyrine.

My white father demanded I be given some form of education. His trips from a wealthy Berlin home to my corner of the damp, crumbling room our family shared were the only protection I had against being forced to mark up my body and begin selling it.

On the cusp of thirteen, I was sent to a utopia of minority rights and representation in comparison to where I had come from; a place where instead of being shoved in ghettos filled with diseases and degradation, I was given the eternal gift of education: the United Kingdom.

Until then, my education had been built by dancing lessons from my ma and grandma under the thick clouds that moved with us. It was one of the very few talents I had. I was good at it.

Conversely, school days in the north of England never held the misty fog of nostalgic freedom for me. It was a confusing, exhausting time full of bullying, frustration and ill-fitting clothes from lost and found. I was placed in classrooms with one or two faces that matched mine. The yellow-blushed skins. The wide noses. The brown of our eyes. The chocolate of our hair. It all matched.

My English skills may have been lagging, but I understood the sneering malice when the other Brown faces would throw 'Pikey' at me. They'd be sitting next to some of the white kids, who would throw 'Paki' at all three of us. Still, I couldn't explain my link to the other Brown kids. I wasn't begging for acceptance, just acknowledgement that

I was also part of their struggle, despite the extra obstacle of being Gypsy.

After leaving my abusive guardians' home, I lived in a Gurdwara, a Sikh temple, for a pivotal time in my mid-teens. It was here, countries away from her, that I connected to Isha in a way that I never could sitting inches from her wrinkled feet back home in Slovakia. It had taken a foreign land that she'd never seen for me to know who she was.

I heard her voice in the crowds of women gathering each week to recite *shabads*. I saw her face in the peaceful expressions of women swaying euphorically to the *kirtan*, the devotional singing of Sikh scriptures. I felt like I was meeting her for the first time, though we were countries apart. She wasn't the stoic fighter selling her offspring on the streets. She was a Holocaust survivor facing the harsh racial bitterness of eastern Slovakia.

Her family had left India's bigotry and ended up in Auschwitz. She left the camps and ended up in poverty.

Now I had left poverty and ended up in limbo.

I was always drawn to the folk tales, songs, memories and pulsating thread-work that warmed my shivering body countless evenings in the bosom of my family.

Peace was the soft sounds of *gaaney* – little bells which hang on orange-red thread tied on ankles and wrists. Even in modern, progressive England, it felt like my impoverished family and murdered ancestors were dancing along with me whenever I heard my bells, as I took another step through this life.

I had been indulging in my *Indianness* by dancing all over the UK at weddings and parties. I had also been to India numerous times as a dancer. I felt just as at home under the nourishing sun as I did under the comforting clouds of the United Kingdom.

Despite treating each job like it was the set of *Devdas* or any other major Bollywood movie, it was small-time work. A handful of girls with off-white complexions who were ethnic enough to know how to move to the music of the land. Each time I was repackaged as a Rajasthani princess with a touch of German exotica whenever I introduced myself as Gypsy.

It never bothered me. I was just grateful to be earning food as a young teen working for a woman who would have pretended we were all Nazi sympathisers if it earned us wages.

During one of these trips, I met other Banjara Gypsies. Through extensive, expensive searching and with only a grainy photograph of my great-grandma to guide me, I found her relatives. They graciously invited me to stay with them for a while. Me, a stranger in all but blood and heart-ache, invited into someone's home without any filthy intention or manipulative expectations.

I declined.

I had moved on up! I was English now! How could I live in the humble *kothia* that were like mansions compared to the dirt I was born in, after living in the upper echelon of elegance that was northern England's council estates? I was eating beans on toast and these ones were eating *roti* and *massar di dhal*.

Please.

So I declined their kind invitation and went back to England. Back to the comforts that I had only known for a handful of years but arrogantly believed to be my new reality. The comforts that my new relatives in India couldn't provide for me. Despite their gentleness, their willingness to know me and their pure love, I felt I was too good for that life now.

The only affection and love I had ever known was when I felt my great-grandma's blood rippling in warmth through my veins with each passing day under the domed roof of the temple.

When I left the Gurdwara, I tried to continue the peaceful path of life I was taught. I left for a new start in the Midlands. Instead, I was raped.

I was attacked by a group of men. It humbled me real quick. The greatest clarity comes when you're forcibly reminded of your place in life. And, lying there barely conscious, ripped open with your blood and their sin dripping all over you, is the ultimate reminder.

It destroyed the garlanded view I had somehow maintained throughout all the horror of my early years in England. I blamed the people I dealt with for injustices – our 'guardians', the immigration lawyers, etc. never the land and its rule. But I lost my faith in this paradise after the police treated me like a cockroach who had been begging for rape.

I was the daughter of a whore.

The descendent of both victims and criminals of the Holocaust.

I ignored the scriptures of compassion and healing for the first few months of my recovery. I was focused on the forgiveness that would await me upon my suicide. And the painless, shame-free harmony that would be the afterlife.

During the months I lay in my bed waiting to get physically strong enough to kill myself, I thought about who I was; who I *actually* was. Not the hypocritical blend of Brown pride and white rage – but what makes me, *me*: what I am good at, what I am drawn to and what I find peace in.

In the Midlands, I was in the midst of the Indian community in a way I'd never before. Sewing with, sewing for and being paid by Punjabi and Hindu women. I understood everything they said. I got the references, having watched the same Indian soaps the night before with the Punjabi friends I lived with. I recognised the food, having eaten more than my fair share before, and much of it being similar to the family recipes my grandma had told me of. I enjoyed the music, having performed to many of the Bollywood songs in low-budget backgrounds and dodgy clubs in India, avoiding sweaty, grabbing hands.

Like my ancestors before me, I was part of their India and their culture.

But, again, like my ancestors before me, I was never fully accepted by them. Even when I spoke in Punjabi with them, or I spoke of traditions we shared, or when I would join in the singalongs, bringing in home-cooked Indian delights – I was always made to feel different.

I tried to tell them all about my beautiful, strong roots. Flying in the Slovakian wind, but trailing through Deutschland tinged with the gold of the German flag, buried in the lands my great-grandma had crossed with her parents and siblings, rooted in the rich soil of the land of the five rivers.

They didn't get it.

I hadn't come directly from India. Neither had my ma, so how could I share their identity? I was too far removed from the 'Motherland'. Not to mention the German heritage that I refused to be ashamed of. To them, Slovakia was my home.

Yes, I was Gypsy, and we have the whole 'wandering, carefree souls' stereotype. But in all honesty, I hadn't ever called anywhere *Home*.

Slovakia? One day, it could be. My family doesn't call Slovakia home. It's a place we fled to in search of healing and comfort after Auschwitz. Instead, we were dumped into landfills and crumbling tower blocks. Can I cherish a country that loathes me and my people? That's a conflict within me that grows each passing day since Brexit and the demonisation of Eastern Europe.

Germany? The closest I've ever been so far. I will defend it and honour it forever. From Berlin to Baden-Württemberg, the beauty, magic and wind of Deutschland are unrivalled. Germany is my father's playground, his one great love.

India? It's not my decision to make. In India, sprinkles of our people are littered through films that require a touch of mystic and seductive energy. The representation is small, maybe offensive to some, but we are there.

England? Can't be. My papers say so, but I can't forget the way I was treated by England when I was a victim or the way I was taken advantage of as an immigrant. I will never hate England and I'll respect it like a stepfather for raising me. I call myself English; I have a British passport. But am I truly at home here? Feeling comfortable here, knowing where I am and how to get to my house from anywhere in this frustratingly beautiful country – is that home? Or is it familiarity?

South Asian spaces in England are hit and miss for acceptance of Gypsies. From being asked about my presence at the Brit Asia Awards in the toilets, DM'd about removing the Indian flag from my Twitter bio and even, hilariously, being accused of cultural appropriation for speaking in a language that I had inherited, I have experienced many microaggressions that underline this fact.

How do you explain it? How do you educate people who seem to want to be oppressed? Because these people who want to police me in the name of 'cultural appropriation' aren't the ones fighting for rights for the Punjabi farmers; they aren't campaigning for the rights of gang-raped girls in India; they can't hold a conversation about caste or the needs of people living in dire poverty in India. And yet they want you to stop speaking a language that your ancestors were speaking in concentration camps before being wiped out.

It's as if we're constantly struggling for something we never asked to be born with. None of us asked for the blood that makes people froth at the mouth, hurt us, abuse us, gas us, isolate us and wish us dead.

Like everyone, we want peace.

Why should my family pretend they aren't Gypsies in the land that birthed us?

Why shouldn't I wear my culture's clothing because of the odd chance someone might be offended and ask me to explain myself?

Why should I explain myself?

The fight for Gypsy rights starts at the very beginning of our journey as a people. It starts from clearly differentiating us from other nomadic groups who share our name but not our oppression, and it eliminates those who brand themselves as 'GYPSY' for clout, or as some kind of hardman reputation.

There are people angry that I'm *excluding* them from their *own identity* by talking about Indian roots, when they want the world to think Gypsy culture is the whitewashed 'documentaries' on television – they don't want that fantasy challenged. They want to be Gypsy because of the reputation they think it earns them. The reality is very different.

My incentive is to make sure my kin who left India did not stand defiantly in vain, refusing to bend to the wills of racists and fascists, proudly representing our Gypsy blood, only to be grouped in a catch-all label that includes anyone with a caravan.

But then, who am I to ask for that? I've spent so much of my life watching, enchanted by the pulsing colour of a culture only half mine.

But my identity isn't mine.

Identity is what others consider us. It's only as valid as those that accept it. I've been assaulted and abused for being ethnic, yet in the United Kingdom my people are classified as 'WHITE'.

My ancestors strumming *sarangi*s, my great-grandma's Punjabi bedtime stories, my grandma draping the flag of the Gypsies on her broad shoulders, my ma teaching me the folk dances of generations ago – all of them fading and dying with each erasure of our true roots.

For recognition, for our blood right and for

those Gypsies who have been slain in the name of racism:

ਅਸੀ ਅਜੇ ਵੀ ਲੜਦੇ ਹਾਂ.

We continue to fight.

ON BEING LOUD
AMMAR KALIA

Listening to anyone learn a new instrument is torture, but there is something particularly painful about the drums. Maybe it is to do with their lack of melody, but the birth of a drummer sounds like the insides of a spinning washing machine filled with bricks; a thundering, clattering rhythm that constantly feels on the verge of exploding.

I was, by all accounts, a very quiet child. My mum told me I was born without crying and that I often used to silently fall asleep. I was, in fact, so quiet that my parents once took me to the doctor, scared that I might be non-verbal or that there was something seriously wrong with me. I have an older brother – seven years older – who filled much of that silence for me. My earliest memories are of him running around the house and arguing with our dad, or singing along to Toni Braxton on the hi-fi.

I also remember him with his tablas, these two gigantic spheres, which he would carefully lift from a tattered black sports bag and place on their sausage-shaped holders. The synthetically floral smell of talcum powder would waft into our living room as he slapped his chubby hands together before sweeping his palms on the coarse goatskins, making the *daya* ring out with a flick of his nail-bitten index finger. I would sit and watch, transfixed by his hands moving with such speed and dexterity to produce the kinds of sounds that would make the pit of my stomach tingle with their bassy resonance, or my molars rattle with their sharp high frequencies. I had only ever seen these hands used for eating or in combat over the TV remote. Now they were utterly new and suddenly useful.

My grandfather had always wanted to be a tabla player, and the drums I watched my brother going to work on each week were his. The tablas were a key part of his Punjabi culture – the drums of celebration wheeled out at every opportunity. Somehow, though, he had never learned to play. Perhaps he had bought them in Kenya as a young man, thinking that one day he would be taught, but instead, the chaos of life had burst into the foreground and he'd had to move his family to England as Idi Amin's racist regime in neighbouring Uganda was beginning to make life as an Indian untenable. He brought the drums with him, and they were swiftly stashed away in the garage of their house in Hounslow, packed among the outgrown bikes and loose ends.

Perhaps it was this frustrated sense of creativity that led my grandad to take such an interest in my brother and me learning the tabla, dusting them off for us as a present. From the age of five, he would take my brother to weekly group lessons at the local community centre, which I joined when I was the same age. We would trundle to the musty hall for our first proper introductions to 'Indian music', away from the wedding dance floors and prayers at temple, while our working parents took the night off.

There was no incense burning, no bright colours, no wafting saris. Instead, we would sit in a wide circle on the dark, itchy carpet, tablas at our knees, surrounded by other, stern-looking South Asian boys. Girls were allowed, but unsurprisingly none tried infiltrating this testosterone-fuelled, pubescent environment. At the top of the circle was Mr Kelly. Kelly was a big man; his taut belly would almost push his tablas too far from reach, but he also had the biggest calloused hands I had ever seen, and when he called out the rhythms he always managed to strike, his greasy shoulder-length hair would sway while he tilted his head to the beat. For an hour each week, my brother and I would sit with the group answering Kelly's calls to *ta, tin, dha, din*, my brother speeding through while my tiny hands struggled to keep up.

I was hitting, but no sound was coming out; this wasn't like the drumming I had seen on TV, tabla maestro Zakir Hussain playing with sitar-wielding elder Ravi Shankar, his hands flying too fast for thought – it was more like slapping a wooden table, dull and redundant. Plus, I had somehow managed to learn backwards, with my dominant right hand playing the bass *baya* rather than *daya*. Perhaps I wasn't loud enough for drumming. Maybe I wasn't Indian enough either, unable to understand the words, rhythms and rituals like the other kids. After a few months, I gave up.

*

There aren't many compelling pages written on the art of drumming. Largely, drummers are relegated to the status of boozy background members in the annals of musical history, content to bash away without another thought for their art or practice. Yet one hobbyist drummer, the *New Yorker* critic James Wood, describes drumming as an act that 'returns us to the innocent violence of childhood', a carefree expression like yelling into the wind.[1] For Wood, drumming is some kind of primal experience, a return to the rhythms that formulated the first language.

Yet my childhood was not one of innocent violence; I was not afforded those privileges. I was reminded daily of the colour of my skin and the traumas of immigrant assimilation. My father would thrust his finger into my brother's face while I watched on, transfixed in silent horror, and he would recite the mantra of all racially abused parents: 'You will have to work twice as hard as any white man in this country.' He would then describe being the only Brown boy at school, being chased home by National Front skinheads and having bricks thrown at him, all to cement in our confused heads that despite being born in this country, we were different and always would be.

In his eyes, to yell, to be carefree and innocent, was to be naive. In fact, it was dangerous. Here, we had to be meek and mild, head bowed, focused only on our own feet and the steady shuffle forward. So when I eventually came to the drum set a year after my failure on the tabla, it felt like a transgression. It went radically against everything we had been taught to be, the good Indian boy I had learned to become.

My beginnings were routine enough. My school was offering heavily subsidised music lessons and although the piano caught my eye, my mum gently suggested I try the drums, as I might be able to use some of that tabla knowledge to get a head start. I signed up, bought a pair of drumsticks and then spent the next six months trying to master the most basic boom-bap drum beat.

It was an aggressive and unhinged sound and I was, of course, awful. At least I was making a sound this time, but the kit was too big. I was splayed out, trying to reach the pedal to control the hi-hat cymbals and the beater for the large kick drum, while my brain struggled to coordinate my limbs separately.

My music taste was also coming into its own around this time. It was the start of the new millenium and, for some reason, that brought with it the arrival of the strange rap-rock hybrid of nu-metal. A genre characterised as much by novelty as it was by talent, one of its leading exponents was the band Linkin Park; my friends and I were obsessed. I desperately wanted to play the relatively simple backbeat to their nihilistic hit 'In the End', a song fuelled by teenage angst and set to a breakbeat-influenced, head-banging groove.

But I couldn't hack it. By this point my parents had mercifully bought damping pads to control the tentative racket of my plastic kit, but I still couldn't bring myself to free up and hit like the controlled whirlwinds of archetypal rock drummers Keith Moon or Ginger Baker. Everything was too tight and my sense of time was entirely warped – each hit of the drum was like a punch to the gut.

What I liked about the drums and what kept me going back to them was their balance between measured control and chaos, since the ultimate function of the drums as the cornerstone of any group is to keep time. The drummer has to be a walking metronome; solid, reliable and willing to stick to the groove. I was not.

I understood the transgression of being loud and how it would forcefully punctuate this sense of groove, but I could not cross that threshold. I had initially wanted to understand the tabla, as I thought that would bring me closer to my heritage. Now, I saw that failure to fit in with an Indian musical culture would not consequently allow me to easily enjoy its opposite: my British existence, my Western music tastes. I was realising that my heritage and identity was going to be somewhere in between; neither in the virtuosic raga nor in the hedonism of rock. So I began to formulate my language behind the kit. That, it turned out, was jazz.

I had first gotten into the genre at around fifteen, my nu-metal phase having soon dissipated into a second-hand appreciation of my brother's love of soul, garage and hip-hop. But jazz became a personal obsession after I stumbled upon Miles Davis' *Kind of Blue*, the gateway record for many fans. It all sounded so effortlessly detached and cool, and yet there was so much depth in their playing; the way Davis' horn cut through the thick silence like a strobe, Coltrane's sax noodling around him like a wreath of smoke, while Jimmy Cobb played the drums as if they had their own song he was seductively teasing out. I looked at the black-and-white session photographs shot by Francis Wolff, co-founder of the pioneering jazz label Blue Note, and the musicians leaning on their music stands, dressed in freshly ironed suits, cigarettes dangling from their hands as they were silently lost in thought. Later, I came across art director Art Kane's 1958 photograph of the era's New York jazz greats, all assembled on the stoop of a Harlem building, like the greatest school photo ever taken. This is the place to be, I remember thinking. And I could picture myself there, since none of them were white.

Before jazz, the only non-white rock musicians I knew were the lead singer from Thin Lizzy and Jimi Hendrix. But they were luminescent, loud and bohemian; there was an excess and self-destructiveness to their existence that I knew nothing of yet. It was the same with going to rock gigs – I would be surrounded by angsty kids wanting to smash each other apart in the mosh pit and lose themselves in each others' sweaty, pubescent bodies. But I just wanted to lose myself in my head and the music.

In jazz, I found all that aggression, confusion and feeling wrested into the amorphous sound of a keening sax or the force of a bass string being plucked; I didn't need a singer shouting their lyrics at me when I could hear the breath of a player passing through their horn, inviting me to fill the gaps in their melodic speech with my imagination. And when it came to the gigs, I felt welcome in the quiet darkness, sitting without being seen and only looking at the musicians engrossed in their show.

Jazz became the perfect rhythmic language for me. It lived in that in-between I inhabited with my existence. It is a music largely made up on the spot, and I was coming to terms with the fact that my life and the lives of many of those who looked like me would have to be continually reinvented in the same ways.

You could call that in-between the diaspora – the patchwork dispersion of peoples from their homeland – and jazz is the perfect diasporic music. It is a music that has itself crossed continents, the product of African-American spirituals translated through slavery and immigration into the freeform genre of jazz. Listen to a jazz group playing, even a solo pianist, and it sounds like different generations of an immigrant family having a conversation around the dinner table; several languages may be spoken, often overlapping with one another, but they all move towards a singular expression of a shared culture.

Listening to a record like Alice Coltrane's *Journey In Satchidananda* was like remembering overhearing my mum speaking Punjabi to her mother; I only understood snatches of their words and phrases, but I still knew what they were saying. I could feel it. Rhythms pass through the diaspora like speech and story, from the incorporation of the raga beat-cycle into jazz, to the afrobeat inflections of jungle, it is all one ineffable yet fundamentally intrinsic part of the experience. And the diaspora is nothing if not resilient, always absorbing these cultures and adapting traditions as it expands.

Another key tenet of jazz that resonated with me was its emphasis on improvisation. In many ways, my life up to the age of sixteen had consisted of adhering to a set of cultural and familial rules – that impetus to be a quiet, good Indian boy, head down and moving invisibly forward.

Then, when I was sixteen, my mum was diagnosed with terminal cancer and given only six months left to live.

What's the point of passing through life meekly and unseen if you're rewarded only with this? I remember thinking.

Why even bother trying?

As she passively went through the gut-churning rounds of chemotherapy, remission and recurrence, I was forced to improvise, lest I be sucked into that nihilistic questioning. I had to try and be like Cobb on the Miles Davis record: loose, adaptable and yet ultimately solid, holding the groove. I had to be attuned to the present moment to stave off the jaws of mortality that threatened to leap forward at any moment. If I let my mind think ahead too much, I wanted to explode; I wanted to be Keith Moon, setting fire to the whole fucking lot.

I just about staved off the abyss, but the inevitable came, and she died on 2 August 2013. If before I had used jazz as a framework of cool sensitivity with which I could try and make sense of my diasporic, confused place in the world, I now realised that it was partly an avoidance. Yes, the improvisation worked well, but something would always be missing if I could not also be loud, if I couldn't let out that need to beat everything around me out.

Like drumming, writing came to me slowly. When I reached the end of my time at school, I thought I would pursue music full time, but those pressures to live out a non-threatening immigrant existence still spoke to me. Music is no way to live, it said, get a real job instead. So writing began as a means to a degree, in that least profitable of subjects: English. Yet, as I spent less time at the kit and more time immersed in the words of others, I began to realise that writing could be a creative expression too – it could be personal and unapologetic. Maybe this could be a means to my voice.

As my course ended and I decided to try for a career in writing, it had become just as important as music and something I could also mediate myself through. Where drumming meant being reactive and living in that slippery present moment, writing meant pausing the present and exploring everything it had to offer in the shape of my sentences. Both fed into each other and became increasingly intertwined.

The last time I played a gig, in November 2019, I took a small solo. Usually, I would let a familiar rhythm unfurl from my muscle memory, letting it build but always retaining an ultimate, comfortable sense of control. This time, though, my limbs took charge before my brain had time to think. I remember the bassist looking at me with equal parts surprise and panic as I built speed, hitting harder and faster until I could feel the kit moving beneath me, the cymbals washing out all other sounds. It would be difficult to come back to the song from this.

I realised that this was what had been missing all along. That the loudness wasn't just a means of being heard in the sense of volume, it was about confidence too. It was about sticking your head up above the parapet and being seen for your difference, and even for all your messiness and mistakes, not in spite of them. There is no innocence in this loudness, no childlike sense of wonder. Instead, these mistakes speak of experience, and sometimes that is the most important thing to be heard. Without them we would only ever be playing the sheet music, we would never grasp and push for more.

I realised that something had been lost in my grandparents and parents' immigration to this country, and it was that notion of striving for more. As a racist society and culture demanded they go about unseen, they turned inwards, towards self-perfection – fear became equated with making a mistake and being heard. Their boisterous, tabla-fuelled celebrations were silenced. Without that striving, though, without my grandfather making a decision sixty years ago to pack up his tablas and his belongings, I would never have ended up here. Without continuing to push for more now, I, my family and my culture will remain stuck.

Drumming is meant to be simple, a loud and freeing expression of your body – like the American poet Walt Whitman's 'barbaric yawp' in rhythmic form. Just look at footage of Keith Moon, limbs flailing wildly as he is about to torch his drumkit with the blurred intensity of a man who has four arms pounding through him. Or Ginger Baker's head of flaming hair bobbing in syncopation to the toms that surround him; jazz drummer Art Blakey beading sweat onto the animal skins, his suit pressed to his flesh through the power of his perspiration. There is no melody or harmony to think of, just the speed of your hands and the kicking of feet.

When it came to his music, Louis Armstrong once said, 'What we play is life.' Playing the drums may just be hitting things, but it has also become my means of redefining life, a way of being heard and of embracing that small yet pre-scient gap between the singer and song, the dancer and the dance. Perhaps now that I have put this to the page, I'll go back to the tabla and at last make a sound. ◐

WHO OWNS A STORY?
SALEEM HADDAD

My imagination was the primary tool I had to survive an unstable childhood. While I spent the first seven years of my life in Kuwait, my family left during the 1990 Gulf War. For the next decade we moved between Cyprus, Jordan, Kuwait and the UAE. It was as if, having been violently uprooted, we never again found our footing, and my adolescence was spent moving from one country to another every several years. To cope with the loneliness and alienation brought about by my family's migrations (as well as my burgeoning homosexuality), I created stories for myself. Over time these stories extended into multi-year narrative arcs involving imaginary friends with names taken from pop stars I read about in the British pop music magazine *Smash Hits*: Claire, Sean, Siobhan, Melanie, Kevin, Stephen. Each of these characters had different superpowers. These imaginary friends kept me company and were an anchor in my otherwise turbulent adolescence.

Despite this protective armour of stories, it wasn't until I moved to Canada at the age of seventeen that I truly understood the power that stories have. It was in Canada where I discovered the power of stories in constructing collective imaginations. There, I saw first-hand how black and white narratives could be deployed for political purposes: to crush the multiplicity of an individual's identity and strip away the humanity of an entire nation of people; to turn millions of worshippers of a single faith into a homogenous dehumanised mass; to whip up fear and hatred to gain support for wars and occupations.

Arriving in the small university town of Kingston, Ontario in September 2001 felt like stepping onto the set of a Hollywood movie. I was there for my first year of university, and I was hoping the campus town would be the backdrop to one of those nineties high-school romantic comedies. Maybe I too could walk down these beautiful leafy streets, hand in hand with my Hollywood boyfriend and our gang of fashionable friends, eating takeaway Chinese from cardboard boxes, listening to Steps and Kylie Minogue and speaking in snappy one-liners.

I was correct about one thing: life did suddenly feel like a movie. But rather than a romantic comedy, I found myself in an action movie. And I was playing the villain. Within hours of the planes crashing into the World Trade Center that September, I was no longer 'gay'. Suddenly, I was an 'Arab'. Classmates asked me questions, looking to me to explain what was happening. After all, I was an Arab. I should be able to explain why *we* did what *we* did.

Until then, it had never occurred to me that I was an Arab. Growing up in Kuwait and Jordan, nearly everyone I knew was Arab. The identity was so implicit – so assumed – that other identities superseded it. In North America, what it meant to be 'Arab' took on a new meaning. As the US government relentlessly assembled its allies to war, so much of the Western collective imagination around the Arab and Muslim world focused on the cultural backwardness of our societies: we were a region of misogynists, homophobes, religious fundamentalists. If we were not hanging gays or stoning women then we were the women getting stoned and the gays getting hanged.

In 2001, I had naively come to Canada thinking I'd have the space to come out and explore my sexuality. Instead I found myself discovering and identifying with this new Arab identity. It was not that I was no longer gay. It's just that my homosexuality was no longer the part of myself that felt under attack. Being Arab in North America meant being labelled by larger forces shaped by military strategies, media representations and national and international politics. It meant having to comment on the state of women's rights in the region, having to reassure people that we did not hate Americans, and explaining the hypocritical global policies that were couched in the shiny veneer of white liberal saviour narratives.

Within this context, I found myself retreating even further into the closet. To exist both as a gay man and an Arab man seemed unfathomable. I felt that in order to come out as 'gay', I would, in some way, have to let something go. Was it my Arabness, perhaps? Or my attachment to family and friends back home? At the time I could not tell what it was I would lose, but I felt the loss viscerally. What I did know, however, was that I could not come out without understanding what it was I was coming out *into*. I was not yet comfortable enough in my sense of self to ensure that I could express myself in a way that would not be warped by this collective story that had developed around Arabs and Muslims.

Storytelling is one of the most potent tools at the disposal of the powerful. It's not as directly destructive as guns and bombs, but its power is insidious and long-lasting. Stories engage the subconscious, constructing narratives and images that last for generations.

In *Orientalism*, the Palestinian scholar Edward Said showed how Western colonial powers constructed stories of 'the East' through literature, art, photography and social sciences to rationalise European colonial interventions as noble, civilising missions.[1] In some cases, sexual morality – or rather, sexual immorality – served as fertile grounds for these 'civilising' colonial missions. One hundred years ago, many European powers saw homosexuality as a sign of backwardness and set about 'correcting' it in the countries they colonised.[2] This is why, for example, so many of the anti-sodomy laws in Asia and Africa were first introduced by European colonial rulers, including many of the anti-gay laws currently in place in the Arab and Muslim world.[3]

To bring this up is not to dwell on history; rather, it is to place the present in its appropriate historical context. Dehumanising representations of Arabs and Muslims as dangerous and backward continue to this day, and are used to justify military interventions, occupations and human rights violations. The Israeli government most notoriously employs this tactic, referred to as 'pinkwashing',[4] as one of its primary tools of propaganda in the Global North to justify its continued occupation. In this story, there is a clear juxtaposition of a tolerant and fun-loving Israel set against a dark and savage Arab world. In this story, Israel is presented as a beacon of progress, a life raft of Western values struggling to survive in the dark, hopeless, barbaric waters of the 'Muslim world', which in turn is rendered an ocean of hatred and fear, death and despair.

In this story, queer Arabs like myself only exist as victims – usually nameless, almost always voiceless. Our images are most notably seen with our hands tied behind our backs, our faces covered in cloth, or else in shaky and blurry YouTube footage as our bodies are tossed off towers. You see just enough of us, but not too much.

It's not just the Israeli government that does this. Across Europe, the media and far-right groups regularly highlight the protection of gender and sexual non-conforming communities as a justification to curb the flow of Arab and Muslim refugees into the continent. The Dutch far-right politician Geert Wilders repeatedly paints immigrants of Arab or Muslim descent as homophobic and a threat to LGBTQ citizens. In the UK, David Coburn, a former MEP from the far-right UK Independence Party, stated in 2015 that the UK should not be accepting refugees because doing so would mean that, soon enough, gay people would be stoned to death in the UK too. The result for many queer Arabs and Muslims is a fragmentation of sorts, a hijacking of our narrative. This was most obviously illustrated in the aftermath of the Orlando nightclub shooting in June 2016.

The bodies of the victims were still warm, and already the first narrative had begun to take shape: the shooter was a Muslim; naturally, it was an act of Islamic terrorism. The next day, Hillary Clinton renewed her vows to bomb more Muslim countries,[5] while Donald Trump reiterated his call for a Muslim ban, and congratulated himself for being 'right on radical Islamic terrorism'.[6] In the media, Islam was once again scrutinised, demonised, and picked apart. And as it emerged that the shooter, Omar Mateen, really did not have any connections to ISIS, nor did he even have a grasp of Middle Eastern politics, and that he had expressed homosexual desires in the past, the narrative coalesced around a new story: that of a self-hating gay man from a culture and religion that would never accept him. In all of this, of course, the victims – mostly queer and from the Latinx community – were washed white and ironed straight. No one wanted to talk about this being a homophobic hate crime against queer people of colour.

For many Arab and Muslim queers across the world, this was a difficult and emotional time. Before we were allowed to grieve for our queer community slain in Orlando, we were first expected to defend the contradictions of our existence, as if hyphenated identities were puzzle pieces that could be easily disassembled and showcased to those desperately searching for their next sound-bite.

But there was another, lesser-known narrative not touched upon by the media: Mateen was a gun-lover.[7] Mateen was obsessed with the NYPD.[8] Most relevant, perhaps, was that for nearly ten years, Mateen was a loyal employee of G4S, a British security company, the largest in the world.[9] G4S, much like Blackwater, are in effect modern-day mercenary armies that feed on the 'War on Terror'. But instead of the story of Omar Mateen, the NYPD-idolising, US military-loving, gun-obsessed employee of one of the world's largest mercenary armies, we were told the story of Omar Mateen, the repressed Muslim homosexual terrorist.

In March 2017, I delivered a lecture at McGill University in Montreal. The lecture was about the challenges of writing from a queer Arab perspective in an environment of widespread Islamophobia and homophobia. A year earlier, my first novel, *Guapa,* had been published, a coming-of-age story of a young gay man in a country undergoing an

Arab Spring-style uprising, and his struggle to find his place in a rapidly fragmenting world. When I finished speaking, a young man from Jordan raised his hand. I recognised the student because he'd been on the same flight as me from London the day before. After the plane landed, he had introduced himself as a Ph.D. student at McGill. He said he was coming to my lecture the next day.

As we waited for our bags, he asked what passport I had. I showed him the British passport in my hand, acquired only a few years earlier after an exhausting and expensive eight-year immigration process. He said that he too was working on getting a foreign passport – Canadian, in his case – and we spoke for a few minutes about the opportunities and ease that a Western passport provides, a familiar and easy bonding ritual for Arab immigrants in the diaspora.

The next day in the lecture hall, he was the first to ask a question.

'Do you think, because you have a British passport, that you have the right to set a story in the Middle East, with a gay Arab protagonist?' he asked.

The question threw me. I felt betrayed – that casual conversation at the airport the day before now seemed like it had been a set-up for a public entrapment. Taking a deep breath, I explained that I had written the novel before I got my British citizenship. And that I happened to be a 'gay Arab' myself, and had lived most of my life in the Levant.

'But do you think that your novel could be seen as silencing other queer Arab perspectives... because your novel has become popular in the West, and someone in, say, Midwest America, might think it *represents* all queer Arab experiences? Some people I know in Jordan don't feel that your novel resonates with their experience specifically...'

His use of the word 'represent' struck an interesting note. With that word, I could feel my novel – a single story – collapse under the weight of the thousands it was expected to carry. I was now caught in a trap. Because by answering his first question, I had accepted his fundamental premise: that fiction – particularly fiction from 'marginalised communities' – must serve a representative function for the story to have any 'value', and for the piece of work to avoid being seen as 'harmful' to the community in question.

Guapa was published in March 2016, mere months before the Orlando attack. After the book's publication, I spent two years touring and speaking about the novel in Europe, North America and the Middle East. I found myself having to be both at the forefront of the novel – to market it as a writer and an openly gay Arab man – while also distancing myself from the book, knowing that neither I nor the novel could ever live up to the expectations of 'representation'.

While touring the novel, I began to notice something was happening: a slow and insidious fragmentation between these two identities of mine – 'gay' and 'Arab' – that I had spent years trying to reconcile in my own writing. For instance, I was regularly asked whether I would be allowed to return to the Middle East and whether I faced any dangers or threats because I was so public about my sexuality. At one event in New York, an interviewer asked me how it felt to be a 'writer in exile'. I had never thought of myself as someone in exile. My family still live in the Middle East, many of my friends do, and I spend about half my time there every year. Whether I had somehow skirted the concept or was just straight up in denial, the identity of an 'exile' was not one I felt at home in.

Many interviews continued in this vein, with well-meaning questions about my safety and the safety of my family. Over time, these questions built a wall, placing my queerness and my Arabness on opposing sides. Doubt crept in. In publishing my novel, had I inadvertently prioritised my queerness over my Arabness? Would I be stopped at the border the next time I went home? Or arrested at an event? And what about my parents? Would my father lose his job? Could it be that I might never see them again? Was I in denial?

The summer of 2016 was boiling and full of rage. Brexit, the shootings in Orlando, the slow creeping of fascism across the world. In June, I attended an event as part of Pride week in Padua, a small Italian university town next to Venice. I arrived the afternoon of my event, and the host took me on a tour. Recounting the history of the city, he told me about the refugees and migrants who had arrived that summer, how many of them were forced to squat in derelict houses on the outskirts of the town, and how the grip of the far right had tightened over recent years, using the presence of these refugees as ammunition.

Later that evening, I was brought onstage alongside a prominent gay politician. We were seated on white inflatable couches on a large outdoor stage. The lights shining on us were so bright it was difficult to make out the faces of people in the audience. The discussion was in Italian, and my interpreter wasn't great. At a certain point, she resorted to simply summarising the discussion, and I suspected she was doing the same with my own contributions. Towards the end of the conversation, the gay politician pointed to me and began to speak. Curious, I nudged my translator.

'He is saying that when it was first announced that you were appearing at this event, the Muslim community in Padua were not happy and wanted to protest, and so he is proud that you are here today.'

'The Muslim community?' I whispered. 'Who is in this community?'

'The Muslim people of Padua,' she replied, looking at me as if I was stupid.

I was asked to comment on this, and for a moment I was left speechless. I dodged the question. But it dawned on me that I had been placed, unwittingly, as a pawn in a larger battle, a battle between two communities I had no connection with. I, an Arab but not a Muslim, was now being asked to comment on how it felt to be exiled from the Muslim community of Padua – a community I hadn't known existed a few moments earlier. More than that, for the first time, I felt unsafe on stage.

The book tour in Europe and North America, and the questions I was regularly asked, left me in an agitated and nervous state as I boarded my flight to Beirut a few weeks after the event in Padua. I had arranged a series of promotional events in Jordan and Lebanon. As the plane took off from Heathrow, I found myself vaguely worrying about my safety. Amman and Beirut, two cities where I had commiserated and celebrated with queer friends, fallen in love, and spent much of my childhood, now seemed foreign to me. Or rather, I wondered whether, in publishing the novel, I had somehow become foreign to them.

The event in Amman was organised by 7iber (pronounced 'heber'), one of the few independent media organisations in Jordan that carry out hard-hitting investigative journalism, and who are unafraid to criticise government policy even as the political space to do so continues to shrink. We agreed to hold the event in Arabic.

The night of the event, the large room was completely packed, with those who were unable to enter standing just outside the door, on the sidewalk, watching from the windows. I gave a reading and then discussed politics, sexuality, and the limits of identity and language with a Palestinian lecturer. There was something about that event that remains with me to this day, four years later. Perhaps it was the ability to speak about the novel in the city where I first fell in love with a man. The city that is home to my grandmother's claustrophobic apartment, and that period of my life which, years later, would inspire elements of *Guapa*.

The event in Amman was the first event I had done in Arabic – a language that was both my mother tongue and also felt foreign to me some-how, given how difficult it was for me, growing

up, to find the right Arabic words to describe my
sexual feelings. But in an unexpected way, the
language created a space to have a frank and
honest discussion about sexuality, language and
gender identity, with a sincerity and depth that I
hadn't found elsewhere. I found myself more
easily discussing certain elements of Arab sexuality without the burden of the weighty political
context that came with the English language. Discussing the novel in Arabic also forced me to
think through the words and terminologies I was
using, forcing me to consider each Arabic word's
context, meaning and history.

This process forced me to carve out a space for
myself within Arabic in which I could describe the
struggles of Rasa – *Guapa*'s main character –
whose struggles had so much mirrored my own.
By doing so, I felt like the process of fragmentation I had been feeling that summer was being, in
some small way, reversed. My story was once
again my own. The morning after the event, I
made my way to the airport filled with hope and
optimism, a lightness in my step, the conversation
having the effect of a tall glass of ice-cold water

in what had otherwise been a boiling hot summer of violence and fear.

When we look at the narrative employed by the Israeli government and the far-right movements in Europe and North America, we see queer Arab lives as nothing more than oppression and pain. We are told that Muslim and Arab societies are fundamentally unsafe for their queer subjects. We are told that as queer Arabs, we do not have a space inside our own communities. Underlying this discourse is a singling out of queer Arab suffering as somehow *unique* or *different* from other forms of suffering.

The truth is that for many queer Arabs, our challenges and our solutions, our struggles and our stories, cannot be disentangled from those of our communities. Our struggles are part of the wider ones our communities face: not just in terms of authoritarianism and occupation, but also in terms of class and the fight against the misogyny that underlies our own toxic cocktail of homophobia.

This is not to downplay the very real difficulties of being queer in the Arab world, and the challenges of having to navigate discourses that argue that queer identities are foreign to Arab or Muslim cultures, or that queer identities are shameful and even Satanic. Nor is it to downplay the very real challenges queer communities face in Arab and Muslim communities, both at home and in the diaspora: the social violence inflicted on trans people and effeminate men; the raids on working-class queer spaces; the absence of protective laws; and the fact that privacy is a luxury afforded only to those who can pay for it.

But, alongside the stories of queer rejection, loneliness, violence and silence, there are stories of queer joy, love, acceptance and resistance. These strands don't just run alongside each other; they are cut from the same cloth. Recognising the complexity of our stories – the way joy and pain, acceptance and rejection can exist within the same moment – is what transforms us from voiceless victims to agents in control of our stories.

When I look back at my process when writing *Guapa*, and what drove me to wake up every morning at an ungodly hour and write down my innermost feelings, I realise that I was driven by the urgent need to tell the truth, as I knew it, in all its shades of grey: to capture those moments where fear and love, joy and sadness, and acceptance and rejection exist side by side in perfect contradiction. And I hoped that in doing so, I would myself somehow begin to understand these messy contradictions that made it so difficult to tell my story.

One issue I am highly sensitive to, as a writer who is queer and Arab and writing in English, is the question of audience. I am often asked whether I wrote *Guapa* with a particular audience in mind. The truth is, for the very first draft, I wrote for nobody but myself. My writing was a balm to soothe my wounds, a way to understand the multitude of contradictory questions swirling in my mind, and I could only write the book if I imagined a world without the social shame that had plagued and silenced me for so long.

But I also knew from the outset that, writing in English from the position of a queer Arab narrator, I was about to dive headfirst into a story that is misunderstood, vilified and manipulated for cynical purposes. Because of this, I was vividly aware of the inevitability of not just one audience, but several audiences. Through various revisions, I read and wrote the novel with these different audiences in mind: a queer Arab audience, a mainstream Arab audience, an audience of Arab activists, as well as different types of Western audiences. Through this, I tried to maintain an awareness of the different situations – whether political, social or cultural – in which my novel was being read.

The novel, a single cultural product, began to operate on a number of different planes, embracing not one single truth but several decentred truths. While centring the queer Arab experience within the narrative, I wrote the novel with an awareness that this experience was travelling within an established Western discourse. My hopes in doing so were that this voyage would mix with this discourse, transform it, subvert it, and make it acknowledge the marginalised, manipulated and forgotten stories of queer Arab lives.

As a writer, I recognise that my words will never be able to stop the massacres happening in Syria, the ongoing ethnic cleansing of Palestine, or bring down military dictatorships like those in Egypt. My words won't create shelters for refugees, nor will they end the wars that made them refugees in the first place. But as a writer, what I can do is to help produce new narratives, new stories and new discourses that can move us beyond simplistic binaries. The point was never to write to change the world. At best, one could write to open up the world somehow, in however small a way. To write through all the powerful narratives that strive to bury your voice. In writing the novel, and in engaging with readers around the world, I found myself discovering, at a visceral, emotional level, how to complicate the black-and-white binaries that political narratives work so hard to entrench.

Fundamentally, no one is going to permit us to tell our stories. As vulnerable groups, as marginalised groups, as misrepresented groups, we can't rely on the goodwill of the powerful to give us our stories back. Instead, it is down to us to take back what is rightfully ours. If we look around and can't see ourselves represented anywhere, that's a sign that we need to get out there and do the telling ourselves, work to create the space outside of the rigid binaries to generate new, emancipatory narratives. In our storytelling, we must ensure that truth must always be our target, empathy our guide, and nuance our strongest weapon. ☾

Parts of this essay are adapted from a series of lectures delivered in Canada in 2017.

MY LOVE IS VAST, BUT SO IS MY DIFFERENCE
NOUF ALHIMIARY

I

PAST

Primrose Hill on New Year's offers a panoramic view of Regent's Park and the rest of London. For free, you could watch every fireworks show around London all at once. So many people gather and sit side by side, in the dark, to watch all the figments of glimmering light down the hill, around the city, up in the sky, displays that you would have to pay to watch from up close.

Coming into the new year, I sat on the wet grass alongside a lover, in silence. I glanced at them and asked myself why I wasn't capable of saying something to alter the painful silence. Much like the fireworks, something about our love felt possible, yet unreachable and faraway. We dated for two years, but tonight it felt as though the pain of things that happened in both the recent and distant past was still here with us. And presently, I was consumed with this feeling that I am gathering parts and figments to make a creature that loved me.

We aren't talking after one of our recurrent arguments, after which we would be drained, and nothing about the onset of a new decade was a reason for either of us to reach for each other.

Our relationship was one in which I learned so much about myself, my ability to grow, the capacity I have for change, my shortcomings, and more specifically, my inability to know where to draw the line. It was in this relationship that I became aware not only of the need to learn who I was, but also of the gruelling work needed to delve deeply into the intricacies of my own shadow.

And so we worked, or at least we tried. We tried to chase an illusive ideal of healthy intimacy, one we didn't grow up witnessing. Equipped with nothing but love and the best of intentions. It seemed simple enough: we both wanted a relationship where we prioritised one another's needs, and put ourselves first, where our self-esteem and independence remained intact, where we reassured one another but maintained full respect for one another's individuality and close relationships with each other's friends and family. But as my parts came clunking onto another's, my intentions couldn't uphold the promise of intelligibility.

We grappled and toyed with this concept; we tried time and time again to begin 'loving each other right'. How could we healthily relate to one another when we felt weighed down with this familiar desire to take the things we loved and pin them down so they'd never leave us? And where did this desire come from?

These questions forced me to delve into a journey of healing the love that I am. And so I let myself dive deeply into the feeling of love I recognised. I wanted to discover the historical roots of my desires, and these enquiries brought me to my roots and the love I grew up with. The love I was taught embodied the struggles and experiences of those who came before me. The example of love I grew up with was undying, it was self-sacrificial, but it was no stranger to the act of hurting. The love I knew as a woman, growing up in Saudi Arabia, was a love that held me tightly in place to keep me safe. And yes, I felt safe, but I didn't know how to negotiate my independence.

Love is passed down to us loaded with various burdens that accumulated over lifetimes of struggle to survive. And in diasporic communities, this often meant that the love we inherited from our parents was one where watched them fight each other, or even us, and seldom did anyone offer much in the way of apologies.

To children that grow up alongside struggle, poverty or displacement, there are very specific epigenetic processes that make us more vulnerable to mental illness – and the same is true of the difficult and turbulent relationships that we had with our parents, or the ones we watched our parents have with one another, or the abusive and unhealthy patterns of behaviour that were left unquestioned or were met with silence.

The love we learned about at the intersection of our multiple ethnic backgrounds is a love so grand, so all-consuming, it knows no limits, and it stops at nothing; but it's also weighed down with the burdens of transgenerational and intergenerational trauma. Yet we young diasporic hopefuls enter into the dating scene burdened with a pristine and un-inclusive cultural model of what a *healthy intimacy* must be and feel like.

II

PRESENT

In the first quarter of 2020, my relationship dwindled from silence to separation. The unspoken discussions left hovering between us were palpable, but never felt urgent enough for either of us to address with one another. During that period, the Covid-19 pandemic hit London, and the whole globe, and we were all forced into necessary isolation.

As I was isolating alone, separated from my family back home, and as I struggled through the turmoil of heartbreak, I began doing inner-child meditations. I spoke to my younger self daily in an attempt to hold space for myself; I imaged her speak to me and I listened to her tell me all that she felt, and I imagined holding her as she cried, and I told her she was safe. I thought about family: my parents, grandparents, and great-grandparents. All the questions I would have had for them, had I let my mind grieve the separation we've endured dealing with differing migration policies. And that was a difficult pain to confront, having been born and raised at the intersection of conflicting domains, multiple languages, opposing cultural ideals, differing priorities and identities; at times it seemed hard to see how they would have understood my priorities at all.

I questioned why I oscillated between needing closeness and solitude, and where my conflicting aggressive need for independence and severe fear of abandonment came from. All of these questions I could trace back to one original point of tension: being caught between homelands and heartlands while belonging to neither and both simultaneously.

I, and others like me, want to fulfil our parents' expectations to pay respect to the compromises they've had to make in their own lives. My mother never finished secondary education, but she'll repeatedly beam with pride as she tells the story of my journey to where I am now, working on my doctorate. At the age of fourteen, my mother had to find opportunities for work in Khartoum to support her family. Knowing the full extent of what she had to sacrifice to give me the life I have today, I can't ever take lightly her expectations of me.

However, and even despite being able to understand the generational significance of my mother's expectations as acts of perseverance and sovereignty, I still oftentimes felt crushed under the weight of them. Like me, many other children of the diaspora are negotiating the weight of their cultural and familial expectations, which stem from a desire for survival, with their desires, whatever they might be.

As I arrived to this awareness, I realised I needed to break the cycle and heal by holding space for myself. I needed to sit back, feel the weight of pain experienced presently and in the past, and reach within myself to discern what my voice truly sounded like, what my needs truly were, what *I* expected. In order to meet another with love, I needed to come up with ideals that reflected my inner desires, accommodated my needs and saw my struggles.

I started to wonder: *What does fulfilling love look like to me?* My voice, my opinion matters. Through radically honest conversations with myself, I realised how much I yearned for uncensored and honest connection with my mother and family members, where we slowly gave voice to feelings we've had, recognising each other's pain and working towards finding out how we might foster increased intimacy and respect with one another.

Nowadays, I find myself lovingly reminiscing about my past lover's kindness: the way they were reliable to their family and friends; their sense of duty and responsibility towards their mother; their love of family and Sunday afternoons with everyone gathered in the small living room, wisps of Arabic coffee and the random Yemeni slang words they threw about.

In trying to find a connection to the notion of belonging in London, and to the UK as a whole, I've come to interrogate how I internalised ideals that kept me on the outside. I realise now that to make sense of my place here, I first needed to accept that I may only ever be on the outside in both realms. That recognition is necessary to bridge the gaps in the ways we, the children of diaspora, have learned to approach intimacy.

Restructuring the ways one learns to be intimate is not easy. That process begins with lovingly holding a mirror, not only to ourselves but to the families and histories that made us who we are, and pouring love onto all our parts until the resistance to openness melts away. A task that can feel impossible at times, especially as I navigate the tiredness of dealing with a post-pandemic world as a twentysomething navigating the city, while simultaneously negotiating the added tensions of being a creative person of colour, and managing the various expectations of my family and culture.

During the process of moving on, it was difficult and draining to think of why I might ever want to put myself at risk by opening up to the prospect of intimacy again. However, as I began to pour into my own cup of love with intentional self-forgiveness and self-compassion, this fear started to change and be replaced with a desire for intimacy with all that exists.

Reconfiguring the ways I've approached intimacy is also pushing me to restructure my relationship to the notion of home. In my journey, I've come to understand that this might not be a place or a geographical location. Instead, what I belong to is a glorious jumble of languages, communities, spiritualities, moments of transience and a powerful desire to be resilient and survive as an act of love. This was my inheritance, and it's the legacy that I carry, wherever I might be. ☾

ON SAYING GOODBYE
TARA JOSHI

My ancestors were from foothills in the shadows of the Indian Himalayas. I like to imagine summers there as my dad – Babba – describes them from his childhood: warm, sun-dappled days spent running joyfully through orchards with his siblings, eating apricots and plums from the trees.

Though my roots are in the mountains and I was born down in Mumbai, I grew up on a small rural island off the south coast of the UK. My parents, of course, had always meant to move back to India eventually – when they got married, Babba had assured his new father-in-law this would be the case. But life, obviously, rarely ends up how you plan it.

In the biting winter when I first visited Babba's ancestral home in the northern state of Uttarakhand, we gathered around a bucket of coal set alight for heat, smoke searing our eyes. I was a child, and in that present moment I thought back again to my family's past: men I had never met in their woollen waistcoats, women and children who looked (sort of) like me in thick jumpers and woven shawls, noses snotty from the cold, white hippies coming to visit and smoke ubiquitous hash, everything black and white, like the photos I had seen. I thought of them gathered around a table, eating mustardy greens, rich black broths made from lentil stock, chutneys of smoky roasted hemp seeds, chewy brown sweets covered in white balls of sugar; acquired tastes I have reckoned with for the past two decades or so.

A lack of jobs, access to healthcare and further education meant family members on both sides dispersed from our villages and towns over the last century, be it to elsewhere in India or elsewhere in the world. There was implicitly some temporary nature to the moves. The intention was always to come back: for a summer, retirement, even a week off work. Now, most of our family no longer lives in Uttarakhand, and seeing one another feels increasingly rare.

It's unclear to me what this means for my relationship with family moving forward. During a recent conversation with someone on a dating app, he mentioned watching his grandfather's funeral back home via video call; I told him my grandfather had just passed away too, and that it was jarring not being with family over in India. This was met with an 'Oh, fuck, I'm sorry to hear that. Were you close?' I did not have an especially concrete answer: 'closeness' is an unwieldy concept when you live far away. It struck me that these are not intimacies normally divulged between people who have never met, let alone digital strangers trying to chirpse – but such is the nature of processing surreal, distant bereavement. We search for connection and intimacy in lieu of those relationships we left on the other side of the world.

For all of us, mortality is something that perpetually lurks like a lingering smoke – but in 2020 it has felt inescapable. From the loss of my two remaining grandparents to the unexpected death of a friend, grief has weighed down my last year like an anvil on my chest.

The *New York Times*'s harrowing coverage of Covid-19 deaths included a piece called 'An Incalculable Loss', with one line that really struck me: 'Among the many indignities, [the virus] has denied us the grace of being present for a loved one's last moments. Age-old customs that lend meaning to existence have been upended, including the sacred rituals of how we mourn.'[1]

The world at large has been forced to learn about the weirdness of grief and mourning when we are unable to be with our loved ones. But even before Covid-19, being with your loved ones to say goodbye, to mourn together, was already something that often couldn't be afforded to those of us who have uprooted; those of us who are immigrants.

And as I try to understand long-distance bereavement, I find myself wondering more and more: is immigration in itself a form of grief?

In the UK, I grew up with the small, tight-knit Isle of Wight desi community, as well as distantly related (but emotionally close) family in London and my British school friends. I was always bemused when Babba would start conversations with the Brown strangers we would occasionally spot on the Isle of Wight. Now I understand that this is how communities are built in places where you are very much the minority.

The idea of moving to India, a foreign place, did not appeal to me when my parents floated the idea. For my Ma and Babba, building a new life had inevitably meant leaving their old one for longer than they had ever intended, not unlike their ancestors before them.

I am fascinated by the link that my family still holds with a place they largely haven't lived in since childhood – by the vast WhatsApp networks for various branches of our Kumaoni family tree, older generations keeping connections alive in spite of the separation of years and thousands of miles. Conversely, when not brought together by our parents, my cousins and I were rarely in touch.

Much of my parents' generation can still speak in Pahadi, the dialect of the mountains. On the rare occasions I hear it, my ears strain to pick through the thick accents of 'chu' sounds to see if there are any words or phrases I might decipher. My Hindi is passable, but our local ancestral language is one that is foreign to me, a dying tongue.

One word I do know is 'Ija' – *ee-ja*. Ija means mother, and for me it meant having my Baadi Ija and Chhoti Ija: my older paternal grandmother (*daadi*) and younger maternal grandmother (*naani*), respectively.

In his novel *Exit West,* Mohsin Hamid writes, 'For when we migrate, we murder from our lives those we leave behind.'[2] Lately I have been grappling with this sentiment a lot. In that initial move my parents made decades ago from India to the UK, did they, in essence, kill the life they left behind? Maybe not for them, but perhaps the decision has left roots to dry up in that old land, leaving me, and those who may or may not come next, untethered, with no tangible connection to India beyond skin, half-remembered culture, and smatterings of language.

It's the strange thing about the death of someone who has always been far away – it's easy to forget they are gone. You become so used to seeing them so rarely that you take for granted them always being there. Both my grandmothers are frequent visitors in my dreams. I wake up confused about whether they're waiting back in India, like they always have been.

I still haven't processed that my grandfather, Babbi, my last immediate root in my motherland, is gone now too – it's raw and new and doesn't feel real, and without family around me it feels difficult to reconcile this. My grandparents were the reason for semi-regular journeys back to India, and trying to look to the future of my relationship with the country feels complicated.

Sometimes I think I will just have to accept India becoming simply a holiday destination, albeit an emotional one, popping in on family members I know less well with the family I have made in the UK, eating all my meals with yoghurt, lemon and green chilli like I'm told my other late grandfather used to.

Perhaps my heritage rests largely in these quirks I have inherited from my family. When someone tells me I have picked up a trait from quiet Baadi Ija, I wonder if this can be true when I have, overall, spent relatively little time with her. Yet I have felt a proximity with both my Ijas throughout my life.

Chhoti Ija wore colourful crepe saris that were bright like her aura; when she had been in good health, she laughed wickedly to warm up a room and danced with me like I was the most precious, abundant commodity. She was brash but warm and deeply caring. Then there was the much more solitary, pensive Baadi Ija, who had been a widow most of her life, romantically yearning for her late husband. Deeply intelligent, her head was always in a book, tenderly underlining poems for me to read; otherwise her life was one of stoically tending to her family. She was overly sensitive, with a wry sense of humour.

The disconnect between my life in the UK and my family in India always felt visceral when I met my grandparents; the goodbyes each time were gut-wrenching, with an echoing, achey internal taunt that this might be the last time I saw those beloved elders, because we normally lived nearly 5,000 miles apart. It's odd reminding myself now that I have officially seen all my grandparents for the last time.

As a kid, I remember reading Jhumpa Lahiri's beautiful novel *The Namesake,* and being so struck by the experiences that seemed to match even slightly with my own. Early on in the book, the immigrant couple in the US receive a letter from back home in Kolkata warning Ashima, one of the lead characters, that her grandmother is unwell: 'Prepare yourself [...] Perhaps you may not see her again.'[3] They install a telephone, too, aware that the calls that come late at night will be from home, and will be bad news.

Back in childhood, I felt sad for my parents when they got those calls in the dead of the night about the passing of family members I did not know so well. But I did not truly understand the weight of being so far away until the early hours of 9 May 2016. I woke up in London to a Facebook message from a not-related uncle who I barely know: at 4.12 a.m. he'd written: 'Sorry to hear that. . .'

I called my parents. Chhoti Ija had passed away, slipping beyond the coma she had been in for quite some time.

Hurriedly arranging for a few days off my barista job, I went to the Isle of Wight. On the train journey home, I felt I was floating, suspended, like nothing was real. She had been ill for most of my adult life, in some shape or form, but even knowing how much she had suffered did not make it easier to see her go. It does not make me turn our last few interactions over and over in my head searching for meaning any less; it does not mean I have stopped clinging to my memories of her in good health, being a child in her company, whether in India or the Isle of Wight.

Our regional Hindu funeral practice is a jarringly quick turnaround that sees the body cremated before the next sunset. It was strange to think Chhoti Ija was physically gone from the earth so soon, stranger still that we could not sit with newly bereaved Babbi and hold his hand over the twelve days of mourning. That February, Ma had tripped and broken her hip. Stuck in recuperation from her initial surgery, she was trapped in the UK when her mother passed away. We cried together on the Isle of Wight.

Lots of people associate 2016 with some kind of loss, to the point where it's almost cloying to make note of it. We tense up knowingly as we recall the legitimising of far-right politics; we sigh remembering the stars who left us. For me, David Bowie's death, particularly, involved tears and diary entries and going to mourn with the dancing crowds down in Brixton, sprinkling glitter on the growing pile of flowers, milk cartons and red peppers.

Collective grief is a powerful thing.

Vague dreams of living in other countries, now

I was done with uni, began to feel more fraught and distant – seeing Ma so small in a hospital bed made me think that surely it made sense to be near my family. Will any of us go and live out new memories in the mountains, or have we already dispersed too far? When my roots wilt away, will I have that familial closeness with anyone?

Family, chosen or otherwise, is a fundamental part of our being.

At the tail end of 2019, I went to India for a friend's wedding in Kolkata. Babba had gone to med school there. It was also the last city he and his siblings had all lived in together before his father had died. It would be a long-overdue family holiday, and he was going to take me to all his old haunts – it's a city that has happy memories for him.

When I arrived in India I learned that, down south in Bengaluru, Baadi Ija was frailer than ever. I thought about her big wide eyes, the stubborn independence that meant she insisted on doing all her own laundry by hand well into her eighties.

It was not a question that we would skip the wedding and go be with her. Cousins and family who I rarely see all gathered together to hold our Baadi Ija's hand, to sing her songs, to help give her chai and mithai. Sometimes, I tried to tell her about my life in weird, English-accented Hindi. After all the times over the years when I had left that bedroom crying, convincing myself I would not see this woman again, it was striking being there and knowing that this was the actual goodbye.

Baadi Ija always laughed remembering her first day looking after me on the Isle of Wight – one of many brief trips she made to the UK over the years, at the whim of the visa system, to help with housework and childcare – when my parents both left for work. Apparently I spent that day screaming, crying at the window, wanting my parents, ignoring the admonishments of someone who I would later discover was probably one of the toughest women I will ever know. Sometimes, sitting in that room with her in Bengaluru, knowing how much pain she was in, I wanted to scream and cry at the window again. I selfishly wondered if it would have been easier to not be there after all.

It is incredibly hard and surreal to be in the room for death – for once, to not be on the other side of the world when a doctor does jarring checks to write a certificate. I couldn't stick around beyond the funeral – that odd, immediate night where we stayed up with Baadi Ija's body as she lay on the floor as if asleep, wrapped in a pristine sari and bathed in a cloud of heady incense; the strange morning where we touched her feet and covered her body in flowers and holy basil before her sons carried her to be cremated. My cousins and I went outside and sat on a step, staring up at the stars.

My life is still in the UK, and my flights were booked and my job was waiting. I flew back to London. I could look up at those same stars, but I was alone.

Not fully alone, admittedly. Friends cooked me dinner, took me for drinks, one even booked me an aromatherapy massage – I am looked after by this community that exists around me, even though they aren't people I can mourn my grand-mother with. Perhaps I am foolish not to try, but the grief feels very personal. There are few people I feel comfortable burdening with the pain I am feeling over someone they do not know – it feels like it would be better to keep it to myself so as not to trouble anyone (this, I am told, is a trait from Baadi Ija).

Forcing ourselves to heal and mend ruptures far from our relations, creating new communities to try and muster that feeling and connection and often unspoken understanding – these are all part and parcel of the immigrant experience.

Something has changed this year, though. My cousins and I have semi-regular video calls and virtual board games. There are other cousins I will message on social media, buas and mamas who I will check in on or vice versa, friends and crushes I am willing to be more open with than ever – sometimes, it feels like I'm building something new.

I'm aware we can't know if life has been better or worse for the decision of moving; it is just different. My parents, like many others, accepted those long-distance relationships and long-distance goodbyes – the tangible sacrifice of uprooting – to secure a better future for their kid. I am grateful for many of the freedoms and luxuries I have been afforded for it. Sometimes I wonder what

life would have been like if we had moved back
– but I guess it doesn't really matter.

And I think again about my grandparents and
their parents before them, moving from our villages
with the idea of home still anchored in their heads.
Babba tells me that when my great-grandfather
returned home from a scholarship in London, he
had to partake in atoning rituals because he had
been overseas – he had to be cleansed from the
corrupting influence of the outside world, or otherwise be ostracised from the local community. I
think of how my parents, now retired, split their
lives between here and India, finally making good
on that promise to Babbi, eternally spread
between two worlds.

I studied history at university, and I know I
have a tendency to fixate on the past: gilding
imagined memory like it's mythology, thinking of
my ancestors in the mountains, thinking of my
parents when they arrived in the UK, thinking of
my own life and repeating moments in my head
again and again as though my existence is some
failed romantic comedy.

bell hooks writes in *All About Love: New
Visions* that young people are afraid of love

because they are afraid of the inevitable pain. I guess that notion touches a consistently raw nerve for me – at its worst, this past year has made me feel more afraid than ever of the all-consuming losses yet to come. But hooks goes on to write about the transformative power of love, and how we have to let go of our grief to move forward, in order to love and be loved fully.[4] I'm realising more and more lately that maybe it's not always useful to look back. I am someone who will always hold the past, but I know it is OK to create new concepts of family, new ways to be in touch, new ways to channel our heritage, new ways to love.

I don't know my ancestral language, but I know the word 'Ija'. Both my Ijas have always been far away, and in death they remain thus. And yet, while I may never go to live in those mountains, I carry both my Ijas with me as I move forward, forging new roots. ☾

GARY IS NOT MY NAME
DHRUVA BALRAM

In my grandparents' house, time stands still.

Memories float through the cracks of unopened drawers, out of the heavy air in the living room. Minutes extend into hours, into days. The nights last entire lifetimes. Daily afternoon naps allow time to jerk forward before the evening wind cools Bengaluru. My grandparents, in a home they've called their own for over a decade, a home they know is their last, bow to no one. Though they age – their bodies losing a Sisyphean battle – time itself is momentarily paused.

As we circle his building slowly, Thatha tells me about the long walks he took as a child, a break from the hours of schooling. The second of four living sons, with another eight lost before the age of five, he was the first to leave the village. Shyly, he whispers how he married my grandmother, meeting her for the first time only once before their wedding day. I can imagine them young, nervous, agitated. After my mother was born, Thatha went to Toronto by himself on 7 November, 1962, subsisting on little over the next four months to bring Patti and my mother over.

While Thatha busied himself with work at the University of Toronto, Patti roamed the streets, her flowing sari and bangled bony wrists catching eyes, turning heads. She was a speckle of colour in a snow-white city. Canada removed national and racial restrictions in the 1960s.[1] In ten years, the country's South Asian community grew from 6,774 to 67,925.[2] Most South Asians then were relegated to the suburbs, cities which have become synonymous with the diaspora culture that prevails there: Mississauga, Scarborough and Brampton. Today, Toronto alone has 995,125 South Asians.

Patti grew up in a family of six siblings in a house that – including extended family members – homed fifteen. She had rarely left the village and never boarded an aeroplane before finding herself in Toronto, with its harsh winds and majestic lake. She had to roam supermarkets and converse in an unfamiliar language, confronted by a new, alien reality. One day, the *Globe and Mail*, Canada's most widely read newspaper, ran a picture of Patti wearing a sari. Her oiled, braided hair down to her hips, she looked disconsolately at my one-year-old mother, who covered a wide grin with a chubby hand. In 1963, Thatha and Patti were a rarity, an up-close specimen for whiteness to observe. My grandparents struggled to find a community here, one that mirrored their own back home.

My grandparents left Toronto in 1964 for New Jersey before eventually going back to India. No one was aware then that the child in the photo would arrive back in Toronto four decades later, on 7 November 2003. And, like her father before her, subsist on little to save enough to bring her own family over.

On the last leg of our journey to Canada, we flew from Vienna. With the lights on the aeroplane dimmed, my father and sister were curled up asleep. Excitement coursed through my twelve-year-old veins; life had radically altered in the last six months. Our family had been approved to immigrate to Canada, four years after my parents wishfully applied. After a series of mundane exit processes that became humorous family folklore,

Mum left the country. Dad packed our lives in New Delhi into two suitcases each, selling and donating most of our possessions. Hurriedly, before the year was over, we left India, severing ties to whatever future we had once laid out.

A young Canadian boy sat across from me in the aisle on the last leg of the journey. Around the same age, we played similar games on the in-flight entertainment, helping each other through difficult levels, a mutual understanding developing. Eventually, we started talking. Through the prism of a child on the cusp of adolescence, he told me what life was like in Toronto: the sports teams and latest trends. In turn, I regaled him with childhood adventures – cricket, football, school life, crime folklore, power and water cuts. Instantly, I knew I had his attention. The stories seemed to animate him, and by proxy, I became an object of fascination.

Quickly, I learned that to entice others to me in this foreign land, I needed to make my backstory more alluring. This behaviour, of exaggerating to overcompensate, became a habit. As I immersed myself within the Canadian education system, desperate for friends, India became a romanticised ideal. Slowly the country unravelled in the minds of others by virtue of my stories: a place of mystique and wonder, rife with poverty. I started to believe the extent of my stories as well – whether or not they contained a kernel of truth.

My recollections of a banal ride to school transformed into a story about a woman giving birth on the street. Lower-class and -caste people were everywhere, painted as beggars who were a nuisance and not leading rich, complex lives themselves. For years I spent my days crafting a version of India for my new Canadian peers. At night, I stayed up late speaking to friends in India on MSN Messenger, exaggerating my life in Canada. I felt myself splitting right down the middle, crafting dual identities to build a whole utopian one. I became obsessed with the ideas of these countries and cultures I had created. Like a stream flowing into a river, fantasy became my reality.

Inside, I was rotting away at the core.

Over time, my mood swings became more frequent. As I entered high school, I drank myself to a stupor most weekends. The prospect of being a stereotypical Indian immigrant boy weighed down on me and then dissipated as I failed classes, skipped entire school days, and was threatened with expulsion – twice.

My parents tried everything: enrolling me in after-school activities, summer sport camps, encouraging me to join more teams, paying for tennis lessons, asking whether I'd like to accompany them on a trip at the weekend. But I grew more distant. The harmony that my parents tried so hard to create at home was disturbed by my presence. I never acknowledged my overt Brownness. I shrugged off the usual remarks, ignored the telltale signs of insidious, casual racism, sitting there quietly as I pleaded to fit in with the aspirational whiteness.

I left India secure in the knowledge that English was my favourite and strongest subject in school. I was eager to impress my new teachers in Canada, Mr Heer in particular, as he taught the subject. Reading my name for the first time, his tongue twisted itself into knots while the silence held within it centuries of colonisation. He looked at me, pointed with one large finger and said, 'Gary.' The name stuck.

This, I allowed myself to believe, was how I was to be treated; how things would be.

In her 2017 essay collection, *Too Much and Not the Mood,* Durga Chew-Bose writes, 'There's a type of inborn initiative that comes from having never been obligated to answer questions about the meaning of one's name, or one's country of so-called origin, or to explain the way you look is generationally and geographically worlds apart from where you were born. Since childhood, there's been an assumption that I owe strangers an answer when they inquire about matters I myself struggle to have words for, let alone understand.'

In high school, I emulated the white teens; the ones who, drunk on the weekends, said the n-word freely and told me I dressed 'white'. The same ones who printed dozens of A4 sheets of paper and stuffed them into my locker with the words 'Thank You, Come Again' typed out repeatedly on them. A reference to Apu Nahasapeemapetilon, a character on *The Simpsons*. It may have felt harmless if not for the other papers, which read, 'Pay Your Taxes If You Want To Live Here'.

When the photos of their act made it onto Facebook, I was tagged in them. The perpetrators were lauded; I stayed silent. Let's be real, I probably liked the photo and laughed along, happy to be an accessory to my own pain. The internet became a constant source of bullying, of noticeably addressing the colour of my skin. Increasingly, I found it hard to reconcile my family's Indian heritage with my Canadian life: I rejected the homemade snacks and cultural items that were ubiquitous as a child and, as my parents offered to make me dosa, or teach me to cook matar paneer, I shied away.

I picked fights on the weekend and privately and publicly shamed my family. I couldn't wrap my head around why we lived in Canada when this idea of India existed in my head, perfectly formed like the first snowfall of the year. So, I attacked my Brownness in the comfort of my own home. I cut my skin with the sharp end of the kitchen knives and scissors, assaulting imaginary physical deformities, which I believed were growing out of me.

In the immediate aftermath, much like the stories I created to appease my white peers, I decided to fictionalise the violent acts I laid upon my body. Convincing myself that I had dreamed it while my body ached, I hid the scars on my body. I cover them now with stories of accidental falls and scrapes. Racialised attacks – whether verbal, online or physical – were absorbed and buried, replaced instead with a desire to be within an exclusionary white space.

I learned how to suppress my emotions; to pander to others while clinging to an idea of a utopia. I was enamoured by my peers, they became fixations of an ideal I was attempting to achieve. Despite this, I craved going back to India, where everything was crystallised in perfection, where happiness was a constant, not a fleeting moment. After years of begging my parents, I travelled to New Delhi for two months. At that point, in 2007, I truly believed that my life belonged there. But I spent the majority of my time that summer speaking to my Canadian friends over MSN and emails, even going as far as to call them on landlines. My parents would later admonish me for these charges, having to pay back various family members and friends.

Returning to Canada, I shamefully hid the fact that only one of the dozens of Indian friends I had spent years speaking to on MSN had met up with me. As the cord that tied me to India loosened, I immersed myself in whiteness in a way I hadn't before. It wouldn't be for several more years that I was ready to scrutinise my strange, toxic relationship to the behaviour of my white peers.

By appealing to what people wanted to hear – the rampant poverty stories, mainly – I started to view India through a prism of violence. Chew-Bose says later in her essay, 'D As In', 'When it comes to my identity, the ways in which it confuses or interests others has consistently taken precedent, as if I am expected to remedy their curiosity before mediating my own. In this way, I've caught myself disengaging from myself, compromising instead of building aspirational stamina. While uncertainty about my future is of course not unique to me, I do marvel at the bounty of hesitation I have acquired over the years because I surreptitiously presumed potential was a dormant thing; that it only functions as a trait others see in me.'

Around the time of my subsequent visits to India in 2010 and 2012, I was introduced to diaspora art, which I consumed ravenously. Here, at last, was a community in which I saw myself reflected. The very aggravations and othering that had populated my psyche were now being laid bare by artists like JusReign and HateCopy. These artists defined how a generation connected: instantly, seamlessly across the world. My attempts at finding a community in Toronto had failed; I knew other Brown people existed, but I had sneered at them, as if stepping away from my culture would help elevate me to some kind of imagined garden of success and wealth.

South Asian identity has always been amorphous, in a constant state of flux. As artists painted South Asia under one dominant narrative, I leaned into stories of whispering aunties, scolding mothers and Bollywood afternoons. Again, I felt myself succumbing to the whims of others, eager to satisfy the portrayal of us through a single lens. South Asian culture at the emergence of social media ubiquity reinforced the narrative I had held for so long in my head: a homogenous, upper-caste, middle-class one that strove to push away the complexities that come with being a South Asian person. By crafting an imagined identity, I had ruefully fabricated parts of my life rather than accepting the particular childhood I had had. By wanting to belong to my own diasporic community, I had taken on the assumption – reinforced by stereotypes whiteness had placed upon us – that the diaspora can be painted by one narrative brush.

In his book *Curry*, Naben Ruthnum writes, 'Inventing a shared past to create a unified diasporic culture is, in part, the project of currybooks, of narratives such as *Bend it Like Beckham*, which are built on easily recognisable touchstone tropes. But the past can't be altered to fit a desire for belonging and solidarity in the present: what people in the South Asian diaspora in the West share is that people looking at us assume that we all come from a similar past and place. But we don't, and there's no need to pretend that we do.'

Communities can be hard to find. This is true especially for immigrants. It's why we cloister together like a school of fish, moving as one through a city's arteries. But within these communities exists a plethora of stories; ones which become increasingly hard to document.

The pictures which remain of Patti and Thatha from their time in Canada are blurry and mostly in black and white. Patti, wearing a sari in all of them, looks forlorn, dejected at another day in a supposed paradise – a direct contrast to the bubbly woman I grew up with in New Delhi. Over the years, Patti and Thatha have allowed me ever so slightly into their past. Recently Patti, in a brave act of admission, recounted how lonely and anxious she felt when she first moved to Canada as a young mother. Unsure of how to raise her child as a twenty-one-year-old, her usual support system remained in India. Patti could turn to no one when juggling multiple tasks, while my mother cried in the background, all in a completely foreign environment.

Eventually, the downstairs neighbour, a Malayalam couple, asked Patti to come over. Mrs Samuel would escort Patti around the city, informing her of the street names, along the way instructing her about which shops to avoid and which markets to go to; a friendly guide to an unknown territory. She made Patti's life warmer, providing company to lean on in troubled times. 'To be first-generation means acquiescing to a lasting state of restlessness,' Chew-Bose writes. But that has been instilled in me: Thatha deciding to leave his village; Mum and Dad leaving in their late forties to start a new life; my sister leaving home at seventeen. I had to follow suit as well, to find my own way. To find a disparate tribe who I could call my own. I had attempted to form it with my white peers in Canada and was left knocking at the door; sure, there were aspects of the diaspora which felt comfortable, but the over-arching narratives I was met with were not ones I felt fully comfortable within. The community I ached for felt non-existent.

Now, here, in London, I have dug a trench deep enough to plant roots. As I sit in limbo, awaiting visa approval, I look to those around me and see aspects of a community. Like Patti finding Mrs Samuel, here, I find guides who have helped build the tent poles of a community: people whose lives spread across continents and countries, travelling to and living in lands only imagined by their ancestors. I have finally now found a community willing to huddle together in the face of an oppressive and fickle white gaze, one which bands together under the umbrella term of *South Asian* while desiring to control our narrative, our stories. I find us in London, in Berlin, in New Delhi, in Melbourne, in Toronto and Amsterdam. I find us in the margins of newspapers, inching our way towards the front page. I find us at parties, at the park, at music festivals around a well-lit midnight shisha. I find us on the bus, in shops, on Twitter, on Instagram. I find us routinely silenced while still shouting ourselves hoarse.

All of us will still face racism, have people refuse to pronounce our names, have our skin colour be marked by hate. We will continue to face harassment, slurs, outright violence and prejudice, yet we will still carry on. We are here, together, forming our own communities across lines of class, caste, race and creed, gathering forces to push back against the systemic oppression that groups us all together.

And I am eternally grateful for all these days, these people, this community, for creating new memories in spaces that we are building ourselves.

Finally, after the scars and the attacks, the spitting and the slaps, it feels like being *me*, being Dhruva Balram, is enough. ☾

REST
KIERAN YATES

My mum worked nights in a hotel. When she came back from work, I would see her sprawled out on the couch, her bony wrist flopped on the side of a worn green-velvet sofa, fingertips gently grazing our grey carpet. The other was draped around her head, dark hair released from a tight bun and falling over her face. The only time my mum ever wore shoes in the house was after a night shift, and I would wake up to see her come back, usually when I was getting ready for school, slicking my hair back in the bathroom mirror. When I heard the keys in the door, I would run down, happily pull her shoes off, and wiggle her 20-denier nylon sheer tights down her legs as she dropped, body in full submission, to the sofa.

In later years, my mum worked nights in a residential home, then as a cleaner, then as a carer. My younger brother's and sister's noisy battery-operated toys adapted to these hours, and became timed to chime outside mum's sleep cycle so no one woke her. She was unwittingly creating tales of fractured rest for us to pass on. It seemed to be inherited in the way that her mum would override sleep to make way for labour, sewing late into the night on her Singer, stitching clothes for white ladies. My nanaji worked nights as a baggage handler at Heathrow airport, his dad worked in our village in Punjab before that. My dad worked unsociable hours in the discount shop Pound-stretcher. Before that, his dad worked milking cows in Punjab at dawn before that, and so the cycle continued.

My mum shared memories with me that took her back to her childhood, a small girl playing quietly with her siblings while her dad slept during the day, secretly trying to make loud noises outside his room so that he would come and pick her up and play. Night shifts often conceal our parents from us, and she was trying to grab some time for herself, unaware that she would repeat a similar pattern with us. Toil is inbuilt into the story of working-class immigrants, and the coding makes its way through generations of our DNA, reminding us that rest is a privilege.

In reality, it is actually more than a privilege, it is a birthright, a survival mechanism and an antidote to ill health. We know that a lack of sleep is bad for our bodies. We know that snatched time deprives us, making way for depression, impaired cognition, obesity, hypertension, type 2 diabetes, strokes, cardiovascular disease (CVD), and premature mortality. The ethnic sleep-gap is well known in research circles and our stories already prove what sociologists gather data to know for certain – that sleep is not enjoyed equitably; that generally, white people sleep better.

One of these studies, published in the US journal *Nature and Science of Sleep* in 2019 showed 'explicit racial/ethnic disparities in sleep health' in Black, Hispanic/Latino, Asian and Chinese communities, all of whom reported worse sleep quality than their white counterparts, with Black subjects suffering the worst. For something that disproportionately affects working-class communities of colour (and that the global policy think-tank RAND Corporation called a 'public health problem' in 2018) it's a wonder there aren't more government initiatives that reinforce the importance of a good night's sleep. Losing sleep creates fractures in our health, cracks which shatter and deepen over years of pressure like vast, desolate canyons where there should be life.

Sleep deprivation is built into how we live, but why? These gaps, it seems, exist by design, to prop up the rest privileged people accumulate as a gift from the toil of countless immigrants that afford so many middle-class white people a restful existence. There are parallel lives being lived that see lifts and floors and fences to lean on as respite, lives where people snatch ten minutes on the bus, lived by people who live in alternative temporal dimensions. Time slows for the tired; things become hazy; our bodies accrue weight; we relinquish control of our bodies. We struggle to be alert to the world, to keep up with the pace of those afforded rest. Time, we are forced to acknowledge, is not experienced by us all equally.

The ethnic sleep-gap is something that requires acknowledgement outside medical research alone, in order to reflect on its broader social and emotional implications. Black women, and women of colour generally, feel this bind acutely, as many of them cater to domesticity and the labour it brings. Our culture sings the maniacal chant that a woman's! work! is! never! done! but allows little support for it. For my mum, and many South Asians, the accusation of being a slovenly woman is one of the worst accusations that can be levelled at you. Women across the world are early risers, women like the ones in my family who wake up early to meet the dawn with hands ready to knead dough, to chop and sweep and prepare. When I would visit my masiji over the summer holidays as a teenager and sleep in, she would see my laziness as offensive and I would wake up to her standing over me, tutting, an apron already smeared with ghee. Sometimes she would, exasperated, use my language back at me – hand on her hips, belly sticking out under folds of cotton, and bellow a question to be answered: 'Why are you always chilling?' I didn't understand her then, but years later I made the connection between her life – being spoken down to on the bus, at work, on the street, by patronising teachers, by union bosses, by GPs, and her idea of laziness. That the privilege to lavish ourselves in rest and reflection, like white women on TV do, is not for us. She was trying to tell me, Kieran, get up – you might be on a summer holiday, but holidays, they don't exist in the real world.

This idea that to experience racism is tiring biological work in itself, which hinders our ability to rest, is ripe for further study. In 2019, I researched this for months, asking different people about it, absorbing studies, calling psychologists, data scientists, sociologists and sourcing articles in magazines long out of circulation. I become aware of the work of Guppi Bola, a UK-based public-health practitioner and interim director at Medact, a charity that aims to end health inequity, who deepens my understanding by making connections I hadn't thought of: that racism robs us of good health by not allowing us to rest, to be at ease in our bodies.

Bola's area of study focuses on migrant populations that move from a 'dominant brown country to a dominant white country' and looks at the connection between this and the impact that discrimination and racism has on the body. 'There's been a lot of research from the US and Canada that shows a clear link between heart disease and circulatory disease in migrant populations as a result of experiencing discrimination,' she explained to me when I asked about where to find more data on the topic. 'And that has been brought up by a rising cortisol output, which is the response your body gives to stress. That can have an impact on things like kidney function and the increase of obesity over time.'

The link between racism and poor health is beginning to be explored beyond anecdotal ideas or factors we might assume are a natural result of discrimination (such as a loss of sleep or anxiety). Take one case study from 2017, when NPR, the Robert Wood Johnson Foundation and the Harvard T. H. Chan School of Public Health asked members of different ethnic groups about 'small indignities that showed uncourteous treatment', including bad service at restaurants. It found a link between these experiences and the rapid development of coronary heart disease. The natural question from a study like this might be to ask how we find pause when so many of our bodies are under attack in ways we can't even comprehend?

There is power in the politics of rest. I think about some of the reasons for this, that it might feel like reclamation because white people have largely enjoyed more of it for longer, that in practical terms it fortifies us to be able to fight. Sometimes that point feels like the simplest one: we need energy to fight, so how do we get there?

Activists talk about bodies holding tension, and I talk to my friends a lot about this idea in relation to how the city makes you shrink yourself. We recognise the muscular contraction that comes from subconsciously halving the size of yourself, like my POC friends who have been told not to 'take up space' in white spaces, women who are routinely steamrolled in various forums in their lives. When I started working as a journalist, overpowered by the dirge of white male voices in rooms, at tables, speaking over me, I would go home and feel puzzled at the soreness in my muscles.

I think deeply about how to hold on to respite. A good start might be rethinking how we shame the notion of idleness in a culture where hyperactive and relentless work is demanded. Capitalism teaches us that we must work ourselves to the bone, that laziness is the enemy of progress. Especially for immigrants, that toil is valorised as being part of the contribution we need to make to exist in countries that our ancestors did not come from.

What we do know is that we are told we must work harder than our white counterparts. We *work hard* to be here; we must make an economic case for ourselves; we must be ready for physical work. Images of Black and Brown toil in the form of nannies or cleaners are woven into our consciousness from childhood: in airports, like my grandfather; or cleaning hotels on night shifts, like my mum.

For anyone who has rolled out of a club in London in the early hours, you see the night-time economy in action – immigrant communities who disproportionately work night shifts leaving, or arriving at work, buying tea or water at little pop-up carts while street cleaners flash their lights. I spent years taking the night bus from raves, sharing the streets with some of them, gazing out of the window, watching the world reset. When people fail to see the link between white supremacy and capitalism, I always think of the sleep-gap as a good example.

*

What does it mean, I ask my partner in 2020, that I will never work enough hours to get everything that is required of me done? That no one will ever be able to pay my value, although I set my own rate? We talk about the relentless work pace of some of our peers, of how the 'rise and grind' cultural trope has, for some, become a parody of a maniacal commitment to work, to enhance clout, and to relentless economic self-pursuit which sees sleep deprivation as heroic. Even during the initial weeks of the Covid-19 pandemic, where terrified Britons who could stay inside did, we were met by well-meaning online optimists that encouraged people to see these terrifying moments as potential opportunities for labour: this could be a perfect time to work on *that book*, or creative project! One particular meme that gained traction saw some half-baked faux inspiration about how Shakespeare 'wrote King Lear during quarantine from the plague'. Months later, we learned that Black, Asian and minority ethnic people died at alarmingly disproportionate rates. Black people in the UK were four times as likely to die from Covid-19 compared to their white counterparts, and South Asians almost twice as likely. Much of this was thanks to socio-economic factors like poor social housing, and the sheer number of immigrant communities who make up frontline workers forced to work throughout the pandemic.

Capitalism relies on this sleep-gap and has tricked us into thinking that sleep is the enemy of success. Consider the aneurysm-inducing neoliberal boast of 'they sleep, we grind' as a declaration of your unrelenting dedication to work. Capitalism, the greedy, all-consuming monster that must be fed, doesn't allow for respite. It is working effectively when it snatches our sleep from us, when it keeps us awake at night, when we watch the darkness turn into light.

The radical idea that we must take time to rest has become popular thought for a generation of immigrant kids who, like me, probably saw a lot of this first-hand from their parents, and then, hell-bent on having something better, experienced it for themselves too. The lie that you could seek respite in the world with a good education and a middle-class job comes undone for people of colour, particularly if you're Black. It's worth noting the extent to which respite in the Black community is certainly most aggressively under attack and how we combat a world where our friends and family can't birdwatch, jog, or play with a toy gun.

Spaces designed for leisure, like galleries, are built on colonial reminders of subjugation, where Black art appreciators have been eyed with suspicion. Police stop Black and Brown people in their tracks on their way to dance. In schools, Black and Brown Muslim children have their leisure time interrogated via the UK Home Office's current Prevent strategy – a policy designed to make teachers agents of the state by flagging up any behaviour deemed 'extremist'. It begs the question, when there is policy in the classroom that promotes invasive and accusatory lines of questioning: Where do you go for fun? How do you gather? That the very image of Brown people praying has been weaponised by some sections of British society while white yoga mums perform aspirational 'Om's tells us something about who is allowed to meditate in peace.

I think about all the times I've heard or experienced bouts of activist 'fatigue' in our communities from those who often find themselves alone in a fight. It creeps in when you confront the reality that the structural change you wish to see, of systemic racism that impacts every part of everyone's life, might not be won in your lifetime. It's exactly the point at which you realise that fighting racism and inequality is a life's work that you feel you might need a lie-down. I message my friends on WhatsApp about this fatigue in the group chat and despite myself, laugh at their reaction. We are all lying in our beds at the same time, not quite audacious enough to call what we're feeling 'burnout' as artists and writers who do jobs we enjoy, and instead we use the term 'at capacity' like too many people squashed into the club, catastrophe imminent. We are pulled in different emotional directions – from occupying spaces to marching in the rain, to mobilising our mutual aid groups, to explaining racism to white co-workers, to diligently picking which hill to die on when met with microaggressions. We find tools to metabolise headlines that make us want to sink into ourselves. One of my friends sends a message in the group: 'life, christ.' Three people respond in real time with a single word: 'Yep.' I laugh about this for days after, and remind myself that holding on to joy is energising.

It is always useful to revisit the work of some of our greatest thinkers on the subject to reinforce how we move forward. In 1988, academic and writer Audre Lorde wrote in her *A Burst of Light: Essays*: 'Caring for myself is not self-indulgence, it is self-preservation, and that is an act of political warfare.' Thirty years later, these words have armed generations of people with language to discuss social justice and the political case for self-preservation. Reflecting on this also shows just how haywire the modern neoliberal concept of self-care has become where individuals are made responsible for their own health, care and joy, but rest allows us to pick up the slack for each other as they indulge in dreamscapes.

Activists have responded to this idea of sleep being restorative and necessary. A few years ago, I read about an exhibition in New York City by activists and artists Niv Acosta and Fannie Sosa. Titled 'Black Power Naps' or 'Siestas Negras', the exhibition created space for the beauty and power of rest for Black patrons. Their artists' statement stayed with me: 'As Afro Latinx artists, we believe that reparation must come from the institution under many shapes, one of them being the redistribution of rest, relaxation, and down times.' In Atlanta, a project known as the Nap Ministry set up installations in urban spaces to facilitate rest and Instagram reminders to lie down. They say that they 'examine the liberating power of naps. We believe rest is a form of resistance and reparations. We install Nap Experiences'. Imagine a world where this was built into the architecture of cities across the globe. To delight in idle time is a new idea for me. I ask my partner, the only person around in the lockdown, about this concept that has become real, filling the house. 'What do you think idle time is?' I ask him. 'I don't know.' He pauses. 'I guess, just to be?' Yes, I think, 'To just *be*'.

I think long and hard about the idea of rest as reparation, inspired by the work of these thinkers. How can we trace what exactly has been snatched from us? When the histories of our communities include slavery or indentured labour, then later zero-hour contracts, exploitative working hours and beyond, how do you make the point that what has been taken from you is more devastating than a few late nights? How do you make the

point about communities in ill health, tired spir-
its, neglected siblings? When communities of
colour are asked to explain relatively basic terms
like white privilege over and over again, it draws
new attention to where labour falls. Once every
few weeks I declare that I have stopped using my
emotional and intellectual time for free and when
people ask me to explain racism, why they've
been transphobic, offensive, stupid, I say I am
saving my energy to teach my future children,
where I think it will be better served. These things
add up.

This notion that our energy is not infinite was
used historically by the Black Power movement to
illustrate the need to seek respite from physical
and structural oppression. This idea provided
some brief respite for communities who were
under attack from the state, living in areas where
things like healthcare, fresh food and housing
were difficult to access (especially for Black queer
communities, of which Lorde was a part). This
reminder was one that is evergreen – that it is that
some things take time to change; that we help
ourselves by helping each other. That corporate
hijacking has been rife in the self-care business is

a truth which itself is fatiguing, but we must see the politics of rest as beyond frivolous commodified self-care or meditation apps. No one is looking at rest as a brief massage and a bath-bomb soak. We are looking beyond, to how we provide care in the form of rest for our communities. We want to see stable employment that allows security, safe housing, cladding that doesn't keep residents up wondering if it will catch fire and kill seventy-two people, policing that doesn't run blood cold, a state that supports us, and communities who optimise care, share food, share childcare, share music, build trust.

As I write, in 2020, global revolutionary action is taking place for those who are pushing back, braided into a history of people who have fought before them. While I type, people continue to march from Minneapolis, Boston, Atlanta, New York, to Paris, Kingston, Amsterdam and London. We are told that we can't rest up. We can't take our foot off the gas, we can't stop – that the radical right-wing political climate has proved time and time again that to take anything for granted is dangerous. It's hard to even write when you don't feel rested in your spirit, but the reality is that the moves forward in social justice can't be assumed safe: they can be toppled at any moment. Where is there time to take stock between destroying and rebuilding?

When we think of where we go to rest, I feel more and more frequently that we must go back. I find solitude and balm in the words of Angela Davis, in the pages of Toni Morrison, the actions of Jayaben Desai.

I find the idea that I am part of a generation who have the desire to be part of a society we can't engage with because we're too busy working reprehensible. I try to gather my energy before I use it to power my 10,000 steps a day, so I can come up with better ideas, so that I'm not too tired to skim-read the fine print, so I'm strong for the fight ahead. I try to work within my capacity. I watch videos of cupcakes being iced, I rub amla oil on my scalp, I listen to Sampha. I dance in the kitchen while the kettle boils until it cools and I have to boil it again. I try and slow down so I can think. I think about how being quiet, listening to the song that activists have sung before, can feel radical. But of course, being still is not easy when the world trembles, or when fury reverberates in your body like fizzing atoms.

If this is anything, it is a call to action to see respite as political, to find it for yourself in a culture that does not award so many of us with the space to rest. We must imagine a future where our communities are not as fractured as our sleep. We must find places to recline; we must build rest into the fabric of our structures. Of employment, education, housing, social work, healthcare and beyond through policy, activism and mobilisation. After all, staying alive to how we are oppressed and staying awake are not the same.

When I see my mum now, the youthful melanin in her skin mistakenly peddles a myth of an easy life, but I see the years of snatched sleep. I think of the children across the globe who read the lines on their parents' faces and see late-night punching in, bill worries or homesickness. (Has anyone ever successfully told an immigrant mum to slow down and relax?)

I see all of my childhood in my mum's face and the way her body moves, and it's why now I'm at my happiest when I see my mum rest after years of fractured sleep. It energises me to find a way that we can build peace into our current and future communities. When I go home now as an adult, I share a bed with my mum and I watch her sleep next to me, one arm, thicker now than it once was, caressing the side of the bed, the other gracefully draped over her face, and I breathe in time with her rising and falling chest. I hold her, and for a moment we are suspended in a place where we transcend the waking labour of life, where we release ourselves into a dream world. I don't know how long I look at her, thinking about when we can find time to rest, how we can work better, what the real solutions to these problems are, and before I know it, the sun rises. ☽

HARAMACY

EPILOGUE
ZAHED SULTAN

In 2018, I had been living in London for just under two years and was invited to perform a live music set in Paris in the hip district of Belleville. The night before my show, I was walking with a friend down one of the city's cobbled paths and noticed an unexceptional pharmacy sign blinking in neon green above my head. Only in this sign, the 'P' of the neon light had blown out. I turned to my friend and belted out, *'How sick would it be to create a night called Haramacy?!'*

And so our story began.

In moving to London and exploring the many nuances the city had to offer, something struck me – how come such a diverse city had so few cross-cultural projects? Especially since 'diversity' and 'inclusivity' were the big buzzwords doing the rounds in art institutions and grant-making organisations.

I unpacked this further and created a programme in the spring of 2019 called. . . Haramacy. The intention was simple: create a safe space for people from different communities to interact with each other through art. In its first year, the programme focused on bringing together artists from Middle Eastern and South Asian backgrounds (both of which I am comfortable with) to collaborate using different creative disciplines (also something I am comfortable with through my multimedia arts practice). Haramacy would act as a catalyst for learning about two cultures and initiate discourse around intersectional issues like race, gender, class and ethnicity that exist within both communities.

The name of the programme, Haramacy, is a combination of the Arabic word *haram* (forbidden) and the English word 'pharmacy', implying a safe, trustworthy space that prescribes the antidote to ailments caused by intersectional issues. I invited ten artists to participate in a four-day residency programme and a performance evening. The group was balanced; between them they had numerous skills and came from backgrounds as colourful as mine. None of the artists had worked together before and almost immediately felt comfortable sharing their stories and vulnerabilities in our studio space and breakout rooms at the Albany in south-east London.

As the days progressed, the comfort flourished into kinship. Interweaving individual disciplines, the artists produced new and bold works to be presented at the performance evening in front of a live audience. To instill this sense of vulnerability, I matched artists beforehand and placed them into groups; only revealing their assignments to them once trust had been established in our meet and greet session.

Artists spent the mornings together in the studio learning about each other's practices and approaches to creating bold performances. In the afternoons, the groups broke out into different rooms at the Albany to develop their projects for the performance evening, supported by an audio-visual production team brought together for the programme.

Thankfully, the performance evening turned out better than even I could have imagined. It proved to be a unique and moving experience for those who attended. The crowd was culturally and ethnically diverse, just like the artist groups. They were engaged and at times taken aback by the multiplicity of the evening, which included a talk on body positivity by Harnaam Kaur and an audio-visual-dance performance by me.

All in all, the programme was challenging, and the hours were long – especially for artists who were not accustomed to performance-based work. Though both proved inconsequential to everyone involved, as the theme was relatable and the opportunity to collaborate while embracing discomfort was welcomed.

From what I experienced through the programme, exploring the often-overlooked heritage of two cultures while celebrating their similarities can create a new, hybrid space that feels comfortable. Like home.

Having completed its third year, the Haramacy programme is building on its original intention, including voices from Black, Indigenous, and People of Colour (BIPOC) communities in its discourse and taking on more bold projects outside of London with artists, students and institutions, among others. In fact, I was so inspired by the programme, I created a combined arts organisation just before the pandemic called COMMUN that focuses on community-building with BIPOC artists.

I have seen first hand how cross-cultural interactions can lead to ingenuity and bridge divides. I have seen it initiate meaningful dialogue and encourage seemingly disparate people to begin to form community.

Collective work is necessary. ☾

EDITORS' NOTE
DHRUVA BALRAM
AND TARA JOSHI

As writers working within the confines of margin-alisation and identity politics, we have long been aware of an obvious gap in Global North media and publishing. We are largely asked to speak on our cultures and our ethnicity only when they are trending and then ignored to write on subjects that aren't deemed topical, even if they have equal importance. We have often been frustrated in not being able to deliver the necessary stories we wanted to read about ourselves, our communities, our friends.

And when we are given space within the white-fronted media world, it always feels like we need to comment on race, on our ethnicity, to defend ourselves from the hatred that surrounds us. It's also the case that a burden of representation exists – when our communities are afforded such little space, the onus to speak for everyone becomes weighty and unrealistic. We wanted to counter that, because we know that to be South Asian or Middle Eastern in the diaspora does not only mean one set of experiences, one narrative brushstroke.

Meanwhile, Zahed's work with COMMUN and Haramacy has been confronting that same gap in the art world, giving voice to Middle Eastern and South Asian voices in the UK, telling cross-cultural stories normally restricted to certain narratives. And so, over coffees and video calls, Zahed suggested we work with him to create a space for ourselves.

We reached out to fellow UK-based South Asian and Middle Eastern writers, journalists and artists whose voices we value. We sought to create a publication to give writers a space to express ideas they felt couldn't fit within industry-standard limitations.

Though the concept was born at the start of 2020, ultimately the publication came together during the Covid-19 pandemic. This is not a collection about the virus, but that context is, of course, inescapable in the ubiquitous impact it has had, and how its multi-layered factors became quickly politicised within all of our communities.

Given the word 'Fracture' as a jumping-off point, everyone dived in.

All the writers involved poured themselves into these essays, their words written while stuck inside, individually combating a new deadly disease and its ramifications. They are the reason this anthology was able to breathe, bringing to life topics rarely discussed outside of WhatsApp group chats, community gatherings and diaspora memes.

For our part, it's been an honour to collaborate with and learn from this multitude of fantastic writers. ☾

CONTRIBUTOR'S BIOGRAPHIES

AINA J. KHAN

is a journalist and writer from West London who has written for *Al Jazeera English*, the *Guardian*, *VICE*, and the *New York Times*, where she became the first International Fellow in 2021. She moved to West Bradford when she was fifteen, and has been straddling the north and south ever since. She worked with Southbank Centre on the first Women of the World (WOW) Bradford festival in 2016, and helped co-found Speaker's Corner Collective, a creative social space led by women and young girls in Bradford. In 2019, she was selected to take part in the BBC Writer's Room, Northern Voices Writers scheme. Her first short play, 'Pashto Thriller', debuted at the Bradford Literature Festival in 2019.

 @ainajkhan

AMMAR KALIA

is a writer, poet and musician. He is a features writer and the Global music critic for the *Guardian*. He published his debut collection of poetry, *Kintsugi: Jazz Poems for Musicians Alive and Dead*, and an accompanying album of original music, in 2020. He is currently working on a second collection, *All Directions At Once*, alongside a series of live performances, as well as his debut novel, *And So Much Longing*. He also writes the agony aunt newsletter, *Stop Trying, Start Crying*. He lives in London.

 @ammarkalia2

CYRINE SINTI

is a writer passionate about Gypsy rights and bringing awareness to the prejudice Gypsies face in Europe. She is Editor-In-Chief of Moonflake Press and has been published in *Crepe & Penn*, *Periwinkle Lit Mag*, *Analogies & Allegories Lit Mag*, *Poetically Magazine*, *Walled City Journal*, *Small Leaf Press* and others.

 @cyrinesinti

DHRUVA BALRAM
is a writer and creative producer. He has contributed to publications such as The *Guardian*, *GQ*, *NPR*, *Crack Magazine*, *Dazed and Confused*, *Mixmag*, *DJ Mag* and *VICE*. He is also the co-founder of Chalo, a not-for-profit organisation which focuses on South Asian culture, releasing curated projects yearly which uplift marginalised voices. Dhruva is also the co-founder of Dialled In, a UK-based company celebrating contemporary South Asian underground culture through mentorship programmes, events and international collaborations.

 @dhruvabalram

JOE ZADEH
is a British-Iranian writer based in north-east England. He writes mostly about culture, philosophy,

and the human experience. His essays and journalism have been published in the *Guardian*, *Noema Magazine*, *VICE*, *The Face*, *Crack Magazine* and *The Fader*.

 @joe_zadeh

KIERAN YATES
is a British-Indian journalist and editor who writes about culture and politics. She has written everywhere from the *Guardian*, the *New York Times*, *VICE*, and appears frequently across the BBC as a broadcaster on Radio 4 and beyond. In 2017 she contributed to the award-winning book of essays, *The Good Immigrant,* and her debut book, *All The Houses I've Lived In*, will be published in 2023.

 @kieran_yates

NASRI ATALLAH
is a British–Lebanese author, screenwriter and producer. He is the co-founder of Last Floor Productions, a company dedicated to the creation of Arab-led and Arab-focused film and TV projects for the global entertainment industry.

He is also Contributing Writer at *GQ Middle East* and a regular guest on the *BBC Arts Hour*. His writing has appeared in *GQ*, the *Guardian*, *Monocle* and *Little White Lies*, among other places.

 @nasriatallah

NOUF ALHIMIARY

is an artist and a PhD researcher at UCL's Institute of Education and visiting researcher at Yale's Women Gender and Sexuality department. Alhimiary's art practices encompass multimedia approaches ranging from photography, video, installation, pedagogy, performance and text. Her interests include girlhood, intimacy, gender performance and digital intimacies and her doctoral research explores visuality and effect in digital visual culture.

 @noufling

SALEEM HADDAD

is a writer and filmmaker of Palestinian-Lebanese and Iraqi-German heritage. His first novel, *Guapa*, was published in

2016, and was awarded a Stonewall Honour and won the 2017 Polari First Book Prize. His short stories have been published in a number of anthologies, including the Palestinian sci-fi anthology 'Palestine +100'. His 2019 directorial debut, *Marco*, was nominated for the 2019 Iris Prize for 'Best British Short Film'.

 @salhad

SANJANA VARGHESE

is a British-Indian journalist, visual researcher, reporter and editor. She has an MA in Research Architecture from Goldsmiths, University of London and has previously written for *WIRED*, *New Statesman*, *The Observer*, *The Baffler* and elsewhere on technology, borders, culture and power.

 @sanjanamv

TARA JOSHI

is a British-Indian writer, editor and occasional broadcaster currently based in London. She was the music editor at *gal-dem* magazine from

2018 to 2022. Her work has featured in the *Guardian*, the *New York Times*, *Rolling Stone*, *Vogue*, *VICE* and more.

 @tara_dwmd

ZAHED SULTAN
is an award-winning multimedia artist, culture producer, filmmaker, and social entrepreneur of Kuwaiti-Indian heritage. His work focuses on the intersection between social justice, technology, and culture and has been presented across various media formats and IRL spaces. He is the founder of a combined arts organisation in the UK and a social impact organisation in Kuwait. Zahed receives particular attention for his audio-visual-dance performances which have been presented internationally.

@zahedsultan

NOTES

THE BALLAD OF THE KANGAROO BANDIT

1   Richardson, Lisa, '"Kangaroo Bandit" hops over racial lines: Bank robber is man of many faces', *Los Angeles Times*, 13 March 2001, https://www.latimes.com/archives/la-xpm-2001-mar-13-cl-36895-story.html

2   *Ibid.*

3   Hall, S., Lecture: 'Race: The Floating Signifier', Goldsmiths College, London, delivered 1996.

4   Anzaldúa, Gloria, *Borderlands/La Frontera: The New Mestiza*, Aunt Lute Books, San Francisco, 2012.

5   The Royal British Legion, a charity that provides support to veterans of the British armed forces.

6   Prior to that, the last known Iranian to visit the village was the Shah of Persia in 1889, who came to see the famous Victorian arms dealer Lord Armstrong in his mansion on the hill, presumably to buy guns.

7   Montgomery, Sy, *The Soul of an Octopus*, Simon & Schuster, New York, 2015.

8   Root, Maria P. P., *The Multiracial Experience: Racial Borders as the New Frontier*, Sage, California, 1995.

9   Rutherford, Adam, *How to Argue with a Racist*, Hachette, London, 2020.

10 Sundstrom, Ronald, *The Browning of America and the Evasion of Social Justice*, Suny Press, New York, 2008.

11 Warhol, Andy, *The Philosophy of Andy Warhol*, Houghton Mifflin Harcourt, Boston, 2014.

SHELTER IN PLACE

1 Zhou, Alvin, 'Magic Chocolate Ball Recipe', *Tasty*, 2019, at https://tasty.co/recipe/magic-chocolate-ball.

2 Kincaid, Jamaica, 'Homemaking', *The New Yorker,* 16 October 1995, https://www.newyorker.com/magazine/1995/10/16/homemaking

3 Lefebvre, Henri, *The Production of Space*, Basil Blackwell, Oxford, 1991.

4 Bratton, Benjamin, '18 Lessons of Quarantine Urbanism', *Strelka,* 3 April 2020, https://strelkamag.com/en/article/18-lessons-from-quarantine-urbanism?dm_i=56 G9,6WC8,1266DO,QFNS,1.

5 Ramsay, Adam, 'Stop blaming ordinary people for the UK's pandemic failures', *Open Democracy,* 28 March 2020, https://www.opendemocracy.net/en/opendemocra cyuk/stop-blaming-ordinary-people-for-the-uks-pandemic-failures/.

6 Public Health England, 'Disparities in the risk and outcomes of Covid-19', 2020, https://assets.publishing. service.gov.uk/government/uploads/system/uploads/attachment_data/file/889195/disparities_review.pdf.

7 Booth, Robert, and Barr, Caelainn, 'Black people four times more likely to die from Covid-19, ONS finds', The *Guardian,* 7 May 2020, https://www.theguardian.com/world/2020/may/07/black-people-four-times-more-likely-to-die-from-covid-19-ons-finds.

8 CABE, 'Community green: using local spaces to tackle inequality and improve health', 2010, https://www.

designcouncil.org.uk/sites/default/files/asset/document/
community-green-full-report.pdf.

9   Watts, Joe, 'Ethnic minority Britons twice as likely to be
unemployed, damning new government study finds',
Independent, 3 October 2017, https://www.independent.
co.uk/news/uk/politics/ethnic-minority-report-theresa-
may-unemployed-black-asian-bame-conservative-con
ference-a7979511.html.

10 Gulliver, Kevin, 'Racial discrimination in UK housing
has a long history and deep roots', LSE, 12 October
2017, https://blogs.lse.ac.uk/politicsandpolicy/racial-dis
crimination-in-housing/.

11 Hackney Council, 'The history of Hackney's diverse
communities', 2020, https://hackney.gov.uk/hackney-
diversity.

12 Boyer, Anne, 'This virus', 10 March 2020, at https://
mirabilary.substack.com/p/this-virus.

13 Robinson, Kim Stanley, 'The Coronavirus and our Future', 1 May 2020, *The New Yorker*, https://www.
newyorker.com/culture/annals-of-inquiry/the-coronavi-
rus-and-our-future.

14 Smith, Zadie, 'Joy', *The New York Review of Books*, 10
January 2013, http://theessayexperiencefall2013.qwrit-
ing.qc.cuny.edu/files/2013/09/Joy-by-Zadie-Smith.pdf.

THE SHALLOWS

1   Aly, Ramy M. K., *Becoming Arab in London: Performa-
tivity and the Undoing of Identity*, Pluto Press, London,
2015, p. 202.

2   Jarrah, Najm, 'The Rise and Decline of London as a
Pan-Arab Media Hub', *Arab Media & Society*, 17 January

2008, https://www.arabmediasociety.com/the-rise-and-de-cline-of-london-as-a-pan-arab-media-hub/.

3   Jaggi, Maya, 'Adunis: a life in writing', *Guardian*, 27 Jan-uary 2012, https://www.theguardian.com/culture/2012/jan/27/adonis-syrian-poet-life-in-writing.

4   Atallah, Nasri, 'GQ Honours Adunis With Our Lifetime Achievement Award', *GQ Middle East*, 7 October 2019, https://www.gqmiddleeast.com/culture/gq-honours-adunis-with-our-lifetime-achievement-award.

ON BEING LOUD

1   James Wood, 'The Fun Stuff', *The New Yorker*, 21/11/10, https://www.newyorker.com/magazine/2010/11/29/the-fun-stuff

WHO OWNS A STORY?

1   Said, Edward, *Orientalism*, Pantheon Books, New York, 1978.

2   Han, Enze and O'Mahoney, Joseph, 'The British colonial origins of anti-gay laws', *Washington Post*, 30 October 2014, www.washingtonpost.com/news/monkey-cage/wp/2014/10/30/the-british-colonial-origins-of-anti-gay-laws/

3   Human Rights Watch, 'This Alien Legacy: The Origins of "Sodomy" Laws in British Colonialism', 17 Decem-ber 2008, https://www.hrw.org/report/2008/12/17/alien-legacy/origins-sodomy-laws-british-colonialism

4   Schulman, Sarah, 'Israel and Pinkwashing', *New York Times*, 22 November 2011, https://www.nytimes.com/2011/11/23/opinion/pinkwashing-and-israels-use-of-gays-as-a-messaging-tool.html

5   '"Americans need to stand together": Hillary Clinton's remarks following the Orlando shooting', *Washington Post*, 13 June 2016, https://www.washingtonpost.com/news/post-politics/wp/2016/06/13/hillary-clintons-speech-following-the-orlando-shooting/

6   Schultheis, Emily, 'Trump gets self-congratulatory after Orlando mass shooting', *CBS News*, 12 June 2016, https://www.cbsnews.com/news/donald-trump-gets-self-congratulatory-after-orlando-mass-shooting/

7   Alter, Charlotte, 'Orlando Shooter Bought Gun Legally, Store Owner Says', *TIME*, 13 June 2016, https://time.com/4367592/orlando-shooting-gun-store-owner/

8   James, Brendan, 'Omar Mateen's NYPD Gear Hints at Counter-Narrative Downplayed by ISIS-Focused Media', *International Business Times*, 13 June 2016, https://www.ibtimes.com/omar-mateens-nypd-gear-hints-counter-narrative-downplayed-isis-focused-media-2381559

9   Laughland, Oliver, 'G4S did not psychologically re-evaluate Omar Mateen after FBI questioning', *Guardian*, 14 June 2016, https://www.theguardian.com/us-news/2016/jun/14/g4s-security-firm-orlando-attack-omar-mateen

ON SAYING GOODBYE

1   'An Incalculable Loss', *New York Times*, 27 May 2020, https://www.nytimes.com/interactive/2020/05/24/us/us-coronavirus-deaths-100000.html

2   Hamid, Mohsin, *Exit West*, Penguin Books, UK, 2018, p. 94.

3   Lahiri, Jhumpa, *The Namesake*, First Mariner Books, New York, 2004, p. 85.

NOTES

4   hooks, bell, *All About Love: New Visions*, Harper
    Perennial, New York, 2000.

GARY IS NOT MY NAME

1   Van Dyk, Lindsay, 'Canadian Immigration Acts and
    Legislation', *Canadian Museum of Immigration,* https://
    pier21.ca/research/immigration-history/canadian-immi-
    gration-acts-and-legislation
2   Buchignani, Norman, 'South Asian Canadians', *The
    Canadian Encyclopedia*, 12 May 2010, https://www.
    thecanadianencyclopedia.ca/en/article/south-asians

Unbound is the world's first crowdfunding publisher, established in 2011.

We believe that wonderful things can happen when you clear a path for people who share a passion. That's why we've built a platform that brings together readers and authors to crowdfund books they believe in – and give fresh ideas that don't fit the traditional mould the chance they deserve.

This book is in your hands because readers made it possible. Everyone who pledged their support is listed below. Join them by visiting unbound.com and supporting a book today.

With special thanks to
Muna Al Mousa
Aruna Sultan

Mishaal A

Ian Abbott

Zara Abdalla

Ismat Abidi

Maryam Aboellail

Bénédicte Aboul-Nasr

Amenah Abouward

Martha Adam-Bushell

Mary Adeson

Farida Affalouad

Aaliya Ahmed

Narzra Ahmed

Sana Ahmed

Shibbir Ahmed

Rahel Aklilu

Faisal Al Hassan

Isra Al Kassi

Aisha Al Saif

Dalia Al-Dujaili

Noha Al-Maghafi

Diana Al-Mahmood

Sumayyah Al-Rashid

Hadeel Al-Shamari

Lucinda Al-Zoghbi

Nuzhah Alam

Saika Alam

Zalan Alam

Rabya Alfadl

Arwa Alfailkawi

Ines Alfano

HJ Ali

Zahrah Ali

Dana Aljouder

Friederike Alm

Nadeen Almubarak

Reem Altamimi

Remona Aly

Anu Ambasna

Shelley Anderson

Jasmine Andersson

Niellah Arboine

Christopher Arnold

Zoë Arschavir

Nyela Asad

Jamie Ashcroft

Holly Ashmore

Joy Aston

Mona Azzam

Lorena B

Alex Bacon

Souraya Baghdadi

Adam Bainbridge

Faima Bakar

Lalita Bala

Jason Ballinger

Veena & Srini Balram

Shoubhik
  Bandopadhyay

Alexander Barbour

Megan Barclay

Nadia Bari

Jennifer Barrow

Aneesha Batavia

Nadia Batool

Laura Beckingham

Jack Beeston

Jennifer Beeston

Faye Behbehani

Anahit Behrooz

Biju Belinky

Emira Benfaiza

Natalie Bennett

Farrah Berrou

Emily Beswick

Jitna Bhagani

Alsasha Bhat

Nikki Bi

Motez Bishara

Alexandra Black

Catrine Bollerslev

Emily Bolton

Jacob Bolton

Julie Bozza

Eishar Brar

Catherine Breslin

Shirley Brierley

Charlie Brinkhurst
  Cuff

Rachel Broderick

Helen Ganya Brown

Stuart Brown

Brian Browne

Matt Bruce

Eimear Burns

Mike Butcher

Courtney Byrne

Jay Calderisi

Adam Callan

Emma Capello

Molly Carter

Maurice Casey

Baz Chambak

Dima Chami

Laila Chamsi-Pasha

Jamie Chandler

Nadia Chelbi

Malcolm Chen

Olivia Cheves

Vinay Chhana

Iqra Choudhry

Ankit Chugh

Lauren Church

Anastasia Colman

Shannon Connellan

Rosanna Connolly

Melody Coomer

Nick Cooper

Trevor Coote

Marieclare Corona

Ben Coulson-Gilmer

Laura Coumbe

Nicola Crean

Eve Cromwell

Neil Cronin

Sammie Crook

Julian Crowe

Kate Curry

Ellie Cusack

Becky Dale

Anuradha Damale

Rupert Dannreuther

Dava & Mike

Beth Davidson

Mariam Dawood

Mikayl Dawood

Samya Dawood

Michael Daye

Juliet de Little

Cicelia Deane

Rachel Dedman

Dela

Milo Delaney

Marina Deluchi

Lily Demir

Claire Denvir

Simar Deol

Arjuna Desai

Divya Desai

Reena Desai

N. Desmaison Lohse

Liz Dexter

Deep Dey

Dharmu &
    Krishnamurthy

Bhanu Dhir

Ioana Diac

Roseanna Dias

Sarah Donaldson

Shanice Dover

James Doyle

Karen Drake

Jessica Drury

Mandeep Dubb

Max Dubiel

Nicola Duffy

Ben Dunn

Nia Edwards-Behi

Jessica El Mal

Nassib El Mourabet

Farah Elahi

Wisam Elhamoui

Imogen Ely

Faye Essa

Ayla Chandni Estreich

Dannii Evans

Hannah Ewens

Alison Eynon

Catherine Fairweather

Natasha Fairweather

Mohammed Fakhro

Fatima Faour

Dorine Farah

Rabaa Faraj

Robert Farhat

Finbarr Farragher

Georgia Farrance

Hannah Fay

Hossam Faz

Peter Fellows-McCully

Kristian Fenwick

Colin Fisher

Charlotte Fitt

Solen Fluzin

Valerie Forrester

Em Foster

Michael Foster

Sophie Francois

Grace Franklin

Garcia Franks

Rosie Freeman

Andy Friedman

Richard Furniss

Leonardo Gada

Kapil Gandhi

Luisa Gandolfo

Jake Garlick

Gaurav

Claire Genevieve

Stacey-Louise George

Eva Georgiou

Terry Georgiou

Sahar Ghaheri

Farah Ghulamali

Penny Gilg

Nali Gillespie

Gus Glaser

Theo Glover

Daniel Gomez

Daniel Gorman

Tim Goudswaard

Jonah Graber

Leah Graham

Lynda Gregory

Judith Griffith

Jade Grogan

Katy Guest

Uzma Gulbahar

Anjana Gupta

Habibah Hafeji

Nour Hage

Amber Hahn

Daniel Hahn

Aidan Hanratty

Sana Haq

Zanub Haq

Chloe Hardy

Robin Hargreaves

Maria Harrington

Angus Harrison

Duncan Harrison

Lucy Haskell

Murat Hassan

Suyin Haynes

Tulip Hazbar

Clara Helbig

Jude Henderson

Kate Henry

Chantal Herbert

Alex Herboche

Philip Hewitt

Benjamin Hindle

Thomas Hobbs

Emily Hodder

Teresa Hopps

Molly Horler

Ruby Hugh

Angela Hui

Riem Ibrahim

Eki Igbinoba

Emily Imamura

Heather Iqbal

Madeleine Jacobs

Jacquie

Alice Jacquier

Ramesh Jaiswal

Hafsa Jalisi

Yasmin Jamaludeen

Saju James

Waleed Jarjouhi

Mishaal Javed

Helen Jeffries

Raquel Jesse

Narinder Jhittay

Aimee Johnston

Nemmy Johnston

Bronwen Jones

Emily Jones

Amita Joshi

Anshul Joshi

Bhagwati Joshi

Rajeev Joshi

Ranjan Joshi

Sunanda & Vinit Joshi

Uma Joshi

Hayley Joyes

Jyothi

Huma Kabakci

Nadia Kablukova

Anuja Kale-Agarwal

Ciaran Kane

Rawan Kashkoush

Uzma Kazi

Becky Kearns

Keerti Keerti

Ursula Kenny

Sorcha Keogh

Mustafa Khabir

Zohra Khaku

Amina Khan

Aryana Khan

Ayesha Khan

Humera Khan

Marwan Khan

Naeem Khan

Sarah Khan

Fozia Khanam

Suhena Khanom

Sarah Khullar

Dan Kieran

Jonathan Kimmitt

Sophie KinghAm

Jennifer Kirby

Aoife Kitt

Sarah Knowles

Katie Knutson

Sarathy Korwar

Katerina Koumourou

Vibha Krishnamurthy

Shahira Kudsi

Megan Lacey

Rob Lake

Rosa Langhammer

Mo Langmuir

Kate Latella

Millie Law

Emilia Leese

Kay Leigh

Anna Lekas Miller

Julia LePla

Jeff Leven

Shanna Linn

Olivia Little

LJ

Henna Lone

Ruth Longfellow

Stephen Longstaffe

Fatima Lopez

Emily Lowe

Michael Lynes

Toby Lywood

Siobhan Mackenzie

Lottie Macnair

Emma Madden

Mae & Edmund

Sabrina Mahfouz

Aneeka Majid

Moon-Moon
    Majumdar

Sahar Malik

Lydia Manch

Steve Mannion

Veruska Mano

Samar Maqusi

Usma Mariam Ashraf

Valeria Mariani

Lauren Marinaro

Lucie Marley

Noah Martin

Rachel Martin

Brittany Matya

Dawood Mayet

Pascale Maynard

Marita McCarthy

Marie McGinley

Sue McGinnell

Susie McIvor

Layla McKane

Ian McMillan

Aidan McQuade

Emilie McSwiggan

Grace Medford

Zayn Meghji

Ana Meisel

Ben Meissner

Grace Mele

Christine Mendonça

Minal Menghani

Anna Mészáros

Mariana MG
Baguenier

Ania Milligan

Lu Miranda e Meca
Figueiredo

Zainab Mirza

Alastair Mitchell

Bryan Mitchell

John Mitchinson

Ali Mitib

Layla Mofrad

Manoucher Mofrad

Timothy Mohun

Pamela Moir

Ken Monaghan

Charlotte Moody

Alastair Moore

Bethan Morgan

Holly Morley

Annalena Morris

Daisy Morris

Katrina Moseley

Julia Muggenburg

Rawan Muqaddas

Aleisha Murphy

Eoin Murray

Nadeem Murtuja

Hannah Mylrea

Arwa Nadeem

Nadjibay

Simran Nagra

Rob Nash

Nathalie

Carlo Navato

Chris Newsom and
  Jasmine Milton

Ciara Ni Chleirigh

Sue Nieland

Suria Nisa

Sarah Noonan

Barry Norton

William O'Brien

Conor O'Donovan

Aodhagán O'Flaherty

Erin O'Halloran

Heather O'Halloran

Sue Oakes

Mugren Ohaly

G Oommen

Elsayed Osman

Camilla Marie Pallesen

Jack Palmer

Jasmin Panesar

G B Pant

Parool

Claire Parsons

Henna Patel

Nasim Patel

Eve Paterson

Ellen Patterson

Thomas Pedersen

Martyn Pepperell

Cynthia Pérez Cortés

Rebecca Phillips

Catherine Phipps

Fei Phoon

Ema Pightling

Harvey Planer

Chris Plutte

Katherine Pole

William Poletto

Justin Pollard

Laura Pollard

Diana Popovska

Stacey Pottinger

Leeona Pour Mirza

Loa Pour Mirza

Clare Povey

Will Pritchard

Taybah Qureshi

Angelina Radaković

Radhika & Jitu

Krish Raghav

Iram Raja

Gita Ralleigh

Jo Ram

Banu Ramachandran

Max Ramsay

Kamal Rasool

Nazanin Rassa

Chal Ravens

Zoya Raza-Sheikh

Uzma Raziq

Katherine Reeve

Kevin Reilly

Amy Richards

Jane Richardson

H Rifai

Lucy Riseborough

Rich Robinson

Sarah Rodwell

Susan Roller

Isabel Ros Lopez

Alice Rossi

Dave Rowlinson

Lisa Rull

Jadey Ryan

Munya Saati

Mariam Sadikot

Natalja Safronova

Riyam Salim

A Sandhu

Sandi

Amandeep Sangha

Héctor F. Santiago

Holly Saunders

Camellia Sayed

Romy Schmidt

Thomas Seal

Gianna Seglias

Anantika Sengupta

Billie Sequeira

Amira Serhani

Asha Sethi

Sara Shaban

Diyora Shadijanova

Nirav Shah

Sharleen Shaha

Habeeba Shaikh

Hashim Shamsi

Ruchira Sharma

Hugh Sharman

Ruth Shave

Vincent Sheridan

Henry Shinkfield

Sophie Shippen

Nikesh Shukla

Holly Shuttleworth

Shruti Shyam

Gabriella Simon

Elise Simpson

Sally Sines

Prabeen Singh

Alexander Smail

Adham Smart

Poonam Sodha

Sonia Sofat

Francesco Soragna

Timi Sotire

Yasmeen Soudani

Noor Soussi

K H South

Meena Sriram

Wendy Staden

Henriette B. Stavis

Gabriela Steinke

Megha Sthankiya

Patrick Sturgess

Rebecca Such

Nader Sultan

Aleksander Sumowski

Amileah Sutliff

Scott Sutton

Shagun Talwar

Naila Tasnim

Genevieve Taylor

Tim Terpstra

Thines

Flora Thomas

Rhys Thomas

Georgia Thompson

Ella Thorpe-Beeston

Jessica Tickell
Miriam Tinberg
Callum Trimble-
  Jenkins
Rita Trivedy
Roland Turnell-Ritson
JoJo Tyhurst
Vivek Vadoliya
Vicki Van Cleave
Lise Vanderpiete
Vidyut Unmesh
  Vardhan
Nikhil Varghese
Silvan Varghese
Shahreen Vayani
Arathi Veilex
BR Venkatesh
Babs Viejo
Adit Vij
Peter Viner-Brown
Manu Vish
Stephanie Volk
Amy Walker

Sir Harold Walker
Ken Wallingford
David Walsh
Sophie Watson
David Wenman
Luzia Whitestone
Seth Whitfield
David Willbe
Jenessa Williams
Nastassja Wiseman
Henry Wong
James Wong
Becca Wright
Jerome Wynne-morgan
Mx. Yaffa
Yultuz Yakup
Carolyn Yates
Joe Zadeh
Amber Zafar
Soraya Zahid
Saif Zeraatian
Cat Zhang
Sally Zlotowitz